T0360702

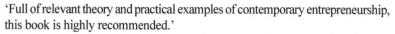

'Full of relevant theory and practical examples of contemporary entrepreneurship, this book is highly recommended.'

Ian Fillis, *Professor of Entrepreneurship, Liverpool John Moores University*

Absolute Essentials of Entrepreneurship

Entrepreneurship is a fundamental business discipline and a phenomenon that drives economic growth globally. This short-form textbook focuses on the absolute essential elements of the field, covering theory and practice.

Illuminating the development of entrepreneurship, the author also concisely introduces the entrepreneurial personality and some of the additional hurdles faced by female and minority entrepreneurs. The central role of creativity, innovation and culture are also examined as well as entrepreneurial strategies for finance and marketing.

This short text provides a unique expert overview for students of entrepreneurship, whilst the practical insights will also be useful in applications for budding entrepreneurs.

Nerys Fuller-Love is Reader in the Business School in Aberystwyth University and has written numerous articles on entrepreneurship in refereed journals.

Absolute Essentials of Business and Economics

Textbooks are an extraordinarily useful tool for students and teachers, as is demonstrated by their continued use in the classroom and online. Successful textbooks run into multiple editions, and in endeavouring to keep up with developments in the field, it can be difficult to avoid increasing length and complexity.

This series of shortform textbooks offers a range of books which zero-in on the absolute essentials. In focusing on only the core elements of each sub-discipline, the books provide a useful alternative or supplement to traditional textbooks.

Titles in this series include

Absolute Essentials of Operations Management
Andrew Greasley

Absolute Essentials of Strategic Management
Barry J. Witcher

Absolute Essentials of Green Business
Alan Sitkin

Absolute Essentials of Entrepreneurship
Nerys Fuller-Love

For more information about this series, please visit: www.routledge.com/ Absolute-Essentials-of-Business-and-Economics/book-series/ABSOLUTE

Absolute Essentials of Entrepreneurship

Nerys Fuller-Love

Routledge
Taylor & Francis Group

LONDON AND NEW YORK

First published 2020
by Routledge
2 Park Square, Milton Park, Abingdon, Oxon OX14 4RN

and by Routledge
52 Vanderbilt Avenue, New York, NY 10017

Routledge is an imprint of the Taylor & Francis Group, an informa business

© 2020 Nerys Fuller-Love

The right of Nerys Fuller-Love to be identified as author of this
work has been asserted by her in accordance with sections 77 and
78 of the Copyright, Designs and Patents Act 1988.

All rights reserved. No part of this book may be reprinted or
reproduced or utilised in any form or by any electronic, mechanical,
or other means, now known or hereafter invented, including
photocopying and recording, or in any information storage or
retrieval system, without permission in writing from the publishers.

Trademark notice: Product or corporate names may be trademarks
or registered trademarks, and are used only for identification and
explanation without intent to infringe.

British Library Cataloguing-in-Publication Data
A catalogue record for this book is available from the British Library

Library of Congress Cataloging-in-Publication Data
A catalog record for this book has been requested

ISBN: 978-0-367-35332-2 (hbk)
ISBN: 978-0-429-33075-9 (ebk)

Typeset in Times New Roman
by Apex CoVantage, LLC

Contents

1 Introduction

Summary

Entrepreneurship is defined as being alert to opportunities, willing to take risks, being creative and innovative and starting a new business. The original meaning of the word entrepreneur is someone who 'takes between,' i.e., buys goods at one price and sells at another, with the aim of making a profit. Other aspects include vision and leadership, independence and being proactive, as well as organising the factors of production. The contributions to the economy includes job creation, innovation and new forms of production and organisation. Entrepreneurship has developed over time from the merchants who took enormous risks to establish trade routes to the very successful technology entrepreneurs today. The entrepreneurial process includes identifying the problem, assessing the market potential and organising the finance and other resources required to start a new venture. The meaning of the term *entrepreneurship* has widened over time to describe anyone who has new ideas and can make things happen in the public and not-for-profit sectors.

How to use this book

This book is intended to provide the reader with a short textbook with the essential elements for the study of entrepreneurship. It includes a simplified presentation of the relevant theories and concepts. Topics included in this text include entrepreneurship theories, entrepreneurial behaviour and personality, female and minority entrepreneurship, enterprise culture, opportunity recognition and entrepreneurial strategies.

The essentials of entrepreneurship are presented in short form by introducing the main themes and concepts in a condensed way. Students, in particular, will appreciate being able to use a short textbook to study for examinations. The structure and scope fits in with the way that the subject is taught in that it is in short sections with tables and illustrations. All the chapters include an executive summary at the beginning and references for additional reading. Other resources, including presentations, are available for lecturers. There are examples/mini case studies in each chapter. Online support is available, including PowerPoint presentations, longer case studies and teaching activities.

Background

Why do we need to study entrepreneurship? Entrepreneurs can contribute to the prosperity of a region and there are many examples of large multinational companies that were started as small enterprises. Entrepreneurship is one of the fundamental elements in all economies. The majority of large multinational companies have started as small enterprises, the vision of one or two entrepreneurs. Successful entrepreneurs can reap financial rewards, as well as being recognised for their achievements and contribution to society. However, there are also many entrepreneurs who operate on a very small scale, barely making a living. Successive governments in the UK and all over the world have policies to encourage and support entrepreneurship. The motivation for making a region or a country more entrepreneurial is to create employment and innovation. Entrepreneurs can also reinvigorate an economy and bring in new ideas and developments.

Entrepreneurship

What is entrepreneurship? There is a general consensus that it is about being innovative, taking a risk and starting a new business. Gartner (1988) defined entrepreneurship as the creation of a new organisation and said that research on entrepreneurship should focus on the behavioural, rather than the personality, aspects. One of the fundamental questions is the relationship between small businesses and entrepreneurship. Although today entrepreneurship has been widened to include large organisation in both the public and the private sector, the main focus is on the creation of a new enterprise. In a small firm, only one person or a small group of people are in control and it is this role that is defined as entrepreneurship.

There is some discussion as to whether lifestyle entrepreneurs, i.e., those who only want to create an income for themselves, are entrepreneurial. Drucker (1993) drew the distinction between small business and entrepreneurship and said that not all small businesses could be considered entrepreneurial. He acknowledged that someone opening a new business such as a restaurant is taking a risk but they are not creating something new, whereas McDonald's created a new method of delivery and a new market.

Table 1.1 Entrepreneurial activities

Arbitrage	Buying goods at one price and selling at another, with the intention of making a profit on the exchange
Opportunities	Alertness to ideas and opportunities
Innovation	Developing new products and services as well as new markets and new ways of production
Raising finance/capitalist	Investing own money as well as raising external finance
New business	Starting and growing a new business and creating new jobs
Risk and uncertainty	Bearing the risk and uncertainty of failure
Forecasting demand	Ability to foresee and create demand for products and services
Leadership	Having a vision and be able to motivate and inspire people
Management	Organising the factors of production and the resources needed
Creativity	Can create something out of nothing
Control	Control over one's actions and time
Vision	Having a long-term vision for the business
Independence	Independent decision making
Proactivity	Initiating action and pursuing a strategic vision
Persistence	Carring on despite setbacks and failure
Profit	Profit is the reward for the risks taken

The meaning has developed over the years. The word *entrepreneur* comes from the French and, literally translated, means 'take between.' This is the original concept of the entrepreneur, as one who buys at one price and sells at another and makes a profit on the exchange. However, the entrepreneur will not necessarily make a profit every time and, therefore, there is an element of risk in each transaction.

However, there has been some consensus of what entrepreneurship entails including those shown in Table 1.1.

Entrepreneurship and economic growth

One of the reasons for looking at entrepreneurship is the contribution to economic development. These include the creation of new jobs, innovation in developing new or improved products and services and new markets. Governments target the small-business sector in the hope that they can reduce unemployment. From the economics perspective, there is equilibrium when supply equals demand at a particular price, and markets are based on this premise. This leaves little room for entrepreneurship and small businesses, as the market would be dominated by large firms, which are more efficient. Economists see entrepreneurship as a response to the inefficiencies of the large firms and the entrepreneur as the co-ordinator of production.

Over the centuries, entrepreneurship has thrived in different parts of the world and at different times. Merchants who crossed the oceans in search of commercial exchange were responsible for building empires and developing regions. Cities were built around the important ports and these traders were richly rewarded for the risks. Parts of the world developed at different times and from the 17th to the 20th century it was the growth of the cities that provided opportunities for growth. The Low Countries in the 17th century focused on international trade and art, Britain in the 18th century with the Industrial Revolution, East Asia in the 20th century and the US in the 21st century with the developments in computer technology and social media.

Although it is possible to identify innovations that have had a major impact, one of the issues in assessing the importance of entrepreneurship to the economy is collecting accurate data. Some of the data used include numbers of self-employed, the numbers of small and medium-sized enterprises, companies registered and deregistered, VAT registrations, number of employees, number of patents registered, etc. None of these provide an accurate indication of the level of entrepreneurship in an economy. There is also the issue of identifying the gazelles, i.e., those that are going to grow and create employment, and how many fail or barely survive. What is clear is that entrepreneurship does play an important role in the economy and there are many factors at play, including the entrepreneurs themselves, infrastructure, culture, as well as government policies.

Case study: Marks and Spencer

Marks and Spencer is a well-established British retailer with shops all over the UK and in other countries. Michael Marks, a Polish refugee, and Thomas Spencer started the business with a market stall in 1884 in Leeds. A man called Isaac Dewhirst lent Marks £5 to start the business. Their market stall was called the Penny Bazaar because everything was a penny (similar in concept to the pound shops today). The business was originally built on selling British-made clothes sold under its own brand. The company had a policy of giving full refunds on its products, although this has now been changed. The clothes had a reputation for being of good quality and value for the money. The company started selling food in 1931.

For discussion

1   How important was the £5 investment to start the business?
2   Why are immigrants more likely to be entrepreneurial?
3   What was its unique selling point?

Exercise

• Discuss the advantages and disadvantages of starting a business with a market stall. Find other entrepreneurs who have a started a business in this way.

The entrepreneur

What type of person starts their own business? What are the characteristics of the entrepreneur? The general perception is someone who exploits a market opportunity and makes a profit. The term *entrepreneur* has been used to cover a wide range of activities, including self-employment, small business ownership as well as entrepreneurial activities in large organisations. Entrepreneurs can also develop new products or services and create new markets as well as new methods of production. They often have to take creative approaches to solving problems due to a lack of resources, especially financial, and they have to find better and cheaper ways of doing things.

New businesses are required to provide jobs, innovate and create the big businesses of the future. The key people in this process are the people who start their own businesses, the entrepreneurs. There are often negative images of these entrepreneurs, of them exploiting their workers and trying to make a quick profit. However, since the 1980s, the contribution that entrepreneurs can make to the economy has been recognised. Baumol (1968) describes the entrepreneur as an innovator who can transform an idea into an economically viable entity. Starting a new business involves personal responsibility, identifying a market opportunity and taking financial risk. However, entrepreneurs, like the small businesses themselves, are very diverse. Their motivations for starting a business also vary.

The entrepreneur is the person who spots an opportunity, raises the money and brings together the people and the facilities needed to start the business. Entrepreneurs are highly motivated people who are willing to take risks and make things happen. They are not always driven by the need to make a profit, although the desire to make money and improve their lifestyle is an important factor.

Entrepreneurs are all different and they each take a different approach to starting their business. The entrepreneur is willing to take risks, but often in a considered way, balancing the risk with the rewards. They often take ingenious ways to overcome obstacles to starting a business. Although entrepreneurship has traditionally been associated with starting and running a business, it is also used, in a more general sense, to describe someone as entrepreneurial in large organisations, in the public sector and in the community.

The entrepreneur is creative and innovative and is able to start a business, develop new projects, raise financing as well as organise and manage the business on a day to day basis. Some entrepreneurs are better at starting a business than running it on a day-to-day basis and they will transfer the management as soon as possible. Other entrepreneurs are happy to keep their business at a manageable level and stay in control.

Entrepreneurs have vision, commitment, passion and tenacity and are able to inject these values into their business. Many small start-up businesses are now household names. Many companies, for example Monsoon, started off with a market stall. The ability to create a team is an important element in the success of these businesses, together with an understanding of the requirements of their customers. However, one of the main characteristics of successful entrepreneurs is that they have not given up when they faced serious problems and some have failed in a previous business before finding success.

Entrepreneurship is seen by successive governments as a way of reducing unemployment. The objective in more recent years, however, has been to identify businesses that are going to grow, rather than encourage everyone to start a business. This is because of the high failure rate of small firms and also because these firms are the ones that are going to create employment.

Although there is a general perception that entrepreneurs are willing to take risks, the entrepreneurs themselves often describe themselves as risk-averse. However, they are generally very self-confident and sure that their idea will work. Possibly they have a different viewpoint to other people in that they are confident that their business will be a success. There is clearly an element of financial risk and, if the entrepreneur's home is used as security for a loan, other people would not be willing to take this risk.

Creating opportunities

The entrepreneur needs to be constantly seeking new opportunities. However, identifying an opportunity is not enough and the entrepreneur also needs to be able to exploit them. In order to make a profit, the entrepreneur needs to identify opportunity where the returns are high enough to justify the investment of time, money and resources.

One of the characteristics of entrepreneurs is their optimism. Some entrepreneurs may be overoptimistic about the potential of their ideas. The high failure rate for new businesses indicates that possibly the entrepreneur's forecasts for sales and profits are often overestimated. However, the overoptimism may be an important element in the entrepreneurial process, as this may make it easier to raise finance and obtain other resources that may lead to success.

In order to transform an opportunity into reality, entrepreneurs also have to have a high degree of motivation. This is because they are going to encounter difficulties and set-backs as they establish their business. McClelland (1961) identified that those with a high need for achievement may be more likely to exploit opportunities. There are also people who work in large organisations who identify opportunities for exploitation and they may develop these within the existing structure.

Entrepreneurship over time

Over the centuries, the term *entrepreneurship* has developed from Adam Smith's capitalist to the wider understanding today of someone who is creative and opportunistic. Originally, entrepreneurs were merchants who bought at one price and sold at another. These merchants developed trade all over the world and all trading took place originally in markets. The perception of entrepreneurship over the years, especially in the media, has changed from the original capitalists who invested in industries (Figure 1.1).

The understanding and definitions have changed over time. Today, entrepreneurship can also be found in the public sector and not-for-profit enterprises. Starting a business in order to make a profit has been an integral part of the definition of entrepreneurship through the centuries. By definition, organisations in the public sector and social enterprises do not necessarily have profits as their *raison d'être*, therefore, although they may have a surplus to invest in their organisations, they do not face risk

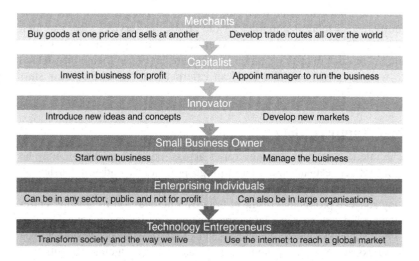

Figure 1.1 Entrepreneurship over time

and uncertainty in the same way as entrepreneurs who have started their own businesses.

The media have often portrayed entrepreneurs as shady characters, ready to focus on making money in the short term. Successful entrepreneurs have a vision and focus on the long term, often with a view of passing on the business to their children. In the television programme *Only Fools and Horses*, Del Boy bottles the tap water in his council flat to sell it as Peckham Spring Water. Although he has many ideas of how to make money, none of them succeed and he only gets rich by winning the lottery.

Entrepreneurs' innovations have changed people's lives. Innovation, according to Drucker (1993), needs to be systematic and does not happen by chance. There are many examples, such as James Dyson, who developed his prototype bagless vacuum cleaner for a number of years before he was successful. Some innovations are often not completely new ideas, but improvements to products or services that were already in existence. There are many entrepreneurs who have taken an existing concept and refined it. An example of this is Mark Zuckerberg, one of the founders of Facebook. The idea was developed by the Winklevoss brothers, but it was Zuckerberg and his co-founders who developed the company into what it is today.

The entrepreneurial process

Entrepreneurs often start by identifying a problem, e.g., James Dyson thought that the existing vacuum cleaners were inefficient and decided to develop the cyclone technology that did not need bags. Once entrepreneurs have identified the problem, they can then see if there's an opportunity, i.e., if there is a market for the product or service. They can then develop the idea and, if it looks feasible, then they can invest their own money or raise finance to start a new venture. They can then either decide to work on their own and build an external team or take on new staff (Figure 1.2).

New venture creation

The rate of new-firm start-ups varies across industries and some may be more attractive than others due to high profitability and low barriers to entry. However, low barriers to entry may increase competition and this may squeeze profits and result in failures. The question of whether entrepreneurship can exist in a large organisation is an interesting one. Drucker (1993) stated that entrepreneurship can be found in large organisations such as Marks and Spencer, although this is based on introducing innovation. It is clear that some entrepreneurial activities exist in large organisations and

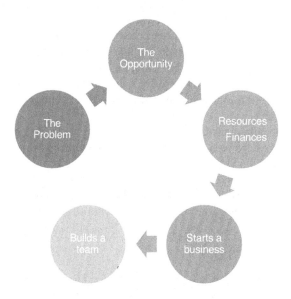

Figure 1.2 The entrepreneurial process

often they are successful if they can mimic the small business and start a new venture within the existing structure. However, the main issue with this understanding of entrepreneurship is the absence of investment and risk. The other issue is that, in order to support and encourage entrepreneurship, governments have to target their support at small businesses.

There are different types of small businesses. There are the entrepreneurial businesses that are innovative and change the existing market structures, and the small-business owners who own the majority of small firms, such as shops and franchisees, and who are happy to run their business on a small scale.

One of the most important functions of entrepreneurship is bringing together the factors of production, including people, and sourcing supplies and equipment. However, the ability to raise finance is considered essential if the business is to grow. There are some examples of firms that have grown without any external finance, including Tetrapak. The majority of businesses will not be able to generate sufficient internal funds, especially in the early stages. Cash is needed both for fixed assets such as equipment, vehicles and premises as well as working capital to purchase supplies and to pay the wages. Many entrepreneurs start a business with their own savings, such as Charles Dunstone, who started CarPhone Warehouse with £6,000 that he had saved in his job as a sales manager.

One of the fundamentals of entrepreneurship, particularly from the economic theory point of view, is profit. Knight (1921) developed a theory of profit based on the entrepreneur buying goods now and selling at a profit in the future. However, he later stated that the profits had to be made over a specific period of time, i.e., an accounting period. From an accounting point of view, profit is the difference between income and expenses and is stated in the profit-and-loss statement that covers a period of time.

Creating an entrepreneurial society is seen as a priority for governments, as new ventures are seen as essential for a vibrant economy. Small businesses are an important source of new jobs. They can also provide jobs for sectors of the workforce that would otherwise find it difficult to find employment, such as young people and disadvantaged groups. New businesses can also diversify the economy and revitalise geographical areas.

Case study: Alan Sugar

Alan Sugar, now Lord Sugar, is now famous for *The Apprentice* television programme, where would-be entrepreneurs compete for the investment to start their own business. He grew up in a council flat in East London and left school at 16 years old. His first business venture was selling beetroots that he had cooked. Later on, he started selling aerials from the boot of a car in the market. By the late 1960s, Sir Alan Sugar had founded Amstrad (the name is based on his initials), which sold hi-fi sound systems and personal computers and word processors. His target market was the lorry driver and his wife who wanted a computer with just one plug. The strategy was to develop electronics at a cheaper price, based on older technology and manufacturing techniques. The first computers and the word processor were a success and this provided the basis for Sugar's fortune. However, subsequent products such as the e-mailer, a combined telephone and e-mailing machine, were not successful. Other products included a gaming console and satellite dishes for Sky and in 2007, Amstrad was sold to BSyB for £125 million.

For discussion

1   Is Sir Alan Sugar a typical entrepreneur?
2   What was his approach to technology?

Exercise

•   Prepare an exercise for the *Apprentice* television show to develop and assess entrepreneurial skills in the candidates.

Entrepreneurial leadership and management

Leadership includes inspiring and motivating people to follow. Some character traits can contribute towards effective leadership and these can overlap with those of the entrepreneur. The meaning of leadership is to decide on the path ahead and supporting and informing followers of the direction in which they are travelling. An entrepreneurial leader will, therefore, be able to communicate the vision for the business and inspire the employees to achieve the overall aims of the business. The term *entrepreneurial leader* is also used to describe a leadership style in large organisations.

The entrepreneur initially has to manage all aspects of the business, and their skills and abilities will have a strong influence on their approach. The aspirations of the entrepreneur, whether they want the business to grow, may also be an important factor. Entrepreneurs usually have excellent soft management skills, such as communication and the ability to sell. However, management skills such as management accounting, managing people, planning and marketing may have to be brought into the business. In the early stages, the entrepreneur will access external networks and advisors to provide some of these skills and, later on, may decide to employ professional managers.

Some of the issues facing small business, such as the high failure rate and that only a small percentage grow to employ more than 50 people, depend on the managerial skills of the entrepreneur. Many entrepreneurs may not be interested in growing their business and are happy to keep it at a manageable level and their main motivation is to provide themselves with an income. Their need for independence and control may make it difficult for entrepreneurs to appoint managers to grow their business. However, successful entrepreneurs are those who are able to build a top team to fill in the gaps.

Poor management, particularly poor financial management, is often the cause of small business failure, especially in the early stage. Short-term cash flow issues or too much debt can cause problems. However, one of the main causes of failure is insufficient sales. This can be exacerbated by poor management on the part of the entrepreneur and by failing to develop other products or services. Entrepreneurs are often overworked and may neglect some parts of the business as they focus on survival.

Drucker (1993) also states that entrepreneurial decision-making can be learnt and that it is behavioural, rather than inherent, and that entrepreneurship is risky because many entrepreneurs don't know what they're doing. One of the keys to successful management in a new venture is to build a management team. According to Drucker (1993), a top management team is necessary before the business grows to the stage that it needs one. This is because it takes time to create a management team because of the need to build-up trust and experience. The problem is that a new venture cannot afford a management team and one of the options is to appoint a nonexecutive director who can help with strategy and decision making.

Entrepreneurship education

Since the 1980s, there has been a huge growth in business and management education. The provision of education in entrepreneurship and small business management developed later and today there are many courses in universities. However, despite the growth in the provision, the percentage of graduates entering self-employment is low. There has been a widening of the understanding of enterprise education to provide management skills to students in higher and further education. The UK government stated in 2018 that enterprise and entrepreneurship education should be available to all students in order to widen their career choices.

The Young Enterprise scheme, started in 1962, is available in secondary schools. Pupils set up their own businesses and generate revenue via sales. The Graduate Enterprise Programme is available in universities and colleges and the Enterprise Programme is also available in primary schools. The scheme is run as a competition, with the regional finalists attending the national final in London.

Corporate entrepreneurship

Although the traditional understanding of entrepreneurship is the creation of a new business, there is also recognition that entrepreneurship can also take place in large organisations. Corporate entrepreneurship is also described as corporate venturing or intrapreneurship. Some large organisations are still managed by the founding entrepreneur and retain some of the entrepreneurial characteristics. Drucker (1993), for example, cites Marks and Spencer as being entrepreneurial. Corporate entrepreneurship can take many different forms, including the creation of a small semi-independent unit within the large organisation. It can also involve commercialising elements of an organisation's activities, for example, parts of the public sector that were previously free of charge. Other examples include Apple's innovation team, which operates in isolation from the rest of the company's activities and reports directly to the top management.

Corporate entrepreneurship can be described as the ability to identify an opportunity that can be exploited. Although the corporate culture will play an important part, it is often one individual who develops the new ideas and concepts. The problem with the innovative employee is that their aspirations may differ from that of the organisation and it may be difficult to reward them fairly. The innovations may also be developed by a team, for example, the design team at Apple who report directly to the senior management. Corporate entrepreneurship may play an important role in developing new products and services and most of the literature on this topic refers to innovation. There are some elements of entrepreneurship that are missing, including the risk and the reward, and it may be the latter that motivates the innovators to leave and start their own business. However, it is clear that corporate entrepreneurship can lead to benefits to the economy, including higher productivity.

Structure and contents

The introductory chapter explains how to use the book and shows how to use additional information. This chapter provides the background on, and an overview of, entrepreneurship, including how the understanding of entrepreneurship has changed over time. The second chapter highlights the development of theories on entrepreneurship including from the economic and other perspectives. The third chapter looks at the personality and character traits of the entrepreneur and the influence of social and environmental factors on the development of entrepreneurial motivation. One of the key success factors for an entrepreneur is the ability to spot a gap in the market and bring together the resources to exploit it in order to make a profit. The fourth chapter examines the process of opportunity recognition. The fifth chapter includes government policies and other support for entrepreneurs and new and growing businesses and the importance of creating an entrepreneurial culture. There has been an increasing interest in female entrepreneurship in recent years and the sixth chapter highlights the issues and developments. Minority entrepreneurship is also included. The final chapter looks at some of the strategies adopted by entrepreneurs, including marketing, harvesting and financing, including bootstrapping.

References

Baumol, W. J. (1968). Entrepreneurship in economic theory. *The American Economic Review, 58*(2), 64–71.

Drucker, P. (1993, 2014). *Innovation and entrepreneurship.* Abingdon, UK: Routledge.

Gartner, W. B. (1988). "Who is an entrepreneur?" Is the wrong question. *American Journal of Small Business, 12*(4), 11–32.

Knight, F. H. (1921). *Risk, uncertainty and profit.* New York: Augustus Kelley.

McClelland, D. C. (1961). *Achieving society* (No. 15). New York: Simon and Schuster.

2 Entrepreneurship
Theories and context

Summary

This chapter looks at the development of entrepreneurial theories from the economics and other perspectives. The definitions of entrepreneurship focus on the behaviour of the entrepreneur, i.e., organising combinations of production, taking a risk and supplying resources not available in the market. The entrepreneur, according to economists, is an intermediary, is a risk taker, is a decision maker, is alert to profitable opportunities and is a catalyst for economic change. The writers about entrepreneurship include Cantillon and Schumpeter. Cantillon defined entrepreneurs as those who did not have a fixed income and could be differentiated from employees. According to Schumpeter, entrepreneurs may have special knowledge that enables them to be innovative and, as a consequence, they are a catalyst for economic change. Kirzner saw the entrepreneur as a middleman, alert to opportunities for making a profit. Entrepreneurs operate under uncertainty and are willing to take financial risks in exchange for making a profit. The theories of entrepreneurship can be divided into two: the behavioural approach, i.e., what the entrepreneur does and the trait approach, which identifies the characteristics. Social entrepreneurship and family businesses are also included in this chapter.

Introduction

Entrepreneurship and small business management is, today, studied all over the world. Entrepreneurship is observed globally in the Global Entrepreneurship Monitor (GEM). The GEM report (Bosma and Kelley, 2019) interviewed hundreds of thousands of people all over the world regarding their attitudes, opportunities and capabilities, fear of failure, entrepreneurial intentions, beliefs and other aspects of entrepreneurship. Aspects such as ease of starting a business, the status of entrepreneurship as a career, opportunity perception, fear of failure and entrepreneurial intentions are included. The countries with the highest level of ease of doing business were the Netherlands, Poland and Sweden.

Although the GEM report has largely focused on early-stage entrepreneurship, the 2018/19 report also highlights the importance of entrepreneurship of all kinds, including mature businesses, family businesses, solo entrepreneurs and gig workers. The GEM report (2019) found that 47% of the entrepreneurs in the survey were motivated by opportunity and 23% were necessity driven.

Definitions of entrepreneurship

- 'Entrepreneurs introduce new combinations of production, notably labour and capital' (Schumpeter, 1934).
- 'Entrepreneurship is about risk, uncertainty, innovation, perception and change' (Hérbert and Link, 1989).
- 'Entrepreneurship is about arbitrage, seizing opportunities and supplying resources lacking in the marketplace' (Kirzner, 1973).

The term *entrepreneurship* has been used to cover a wide range of activities including self-employment, small businesses and entrepreneurial activities in large organisations. However, the most common understanding of the role of the entrepreneur is the person who creates a new business. The word *entrepreneur* comes from the French language and means to 'take between.' This meaning comes from the role of the entrepreneur as a middleman, buying at one price and selling at another. An entrepreneur may have special knowledge or a combination of knowledge or a different interpretation of events.

Adam Smith saw the entrepreneur as a capitalist and that the profits that resulted from running a business were the rewards for risking capital. Therefore, entrepreneurs are risk takers who invest in their own business and are rewarded accordingly.

Case study: the White Company

Chrissie Rucker founded the White Company in 1994. She had a 'light bulb' moment when she went shopping for some crisp white towels and sheets. Her then boyfriend, who later became her husband, had just bought a house and she wanted to impress him and show what an excellent wife she would make. She found a gap in the market between the cheap but poor-quality sheets and the expensive, upmarket bed linen, with nothing in between. When she went to check out the expensive range in a department store, the shop assistant directed her towards the cheaper sheets. She told her sister-in-law, who had also be shopping for white kitchenware, about the experience and Susie responded saying, 'Wouldn't it be brilliant if there was a company that just sold white things?'

From the moment Chrissie had the idea, she became passionate about it and she started saving from her salary as a beauty assistant at a magazine. Her market research included phoning up shops asking how much of the bed linen they sold was white; this gave her the information she needed. She approached the factories that produced the designer brands and decided to sell directly to the customer so that the price would be lower. The company still sells mainly white bed linen as well as other items and sells both online and through high street shops.

For discussion

1 How did Chrissie find the gap in the market?
2 What motivated Chrissie to give her job to start the White Company?

Exercise

• Think of a product that is not available in the shops or online that you have been looking for but didn't find exactly what you wanted at the right price.

The example of the White Company illustrates how entrepreneurs spot a gap in the market. Once the entrepreneur has spotted the gap and started a business to exploit it, it is obvious. However, although other people may have been looking for the similar items, Chrissie was motivated to start a business. She had a role model in her boyfriend, who had started his own business making shirts.

Research into entrepreneurship

Economists looked at the role of the entrepreneur in the economy and described them as a capitalist and a risk-taker, bringing factors of production together to make a profit. Economists have looked at the benefits of entrepreneurship in the economy, such as innovation and job creation, and the role of the entrepreneur as being alert to opportunities to make a profit, a risk-taker and bringing factors of production together. Sociologists have examined the social and psychological factors and their impact on the entrepreneurial personality. Other researchers have looked at leadership and management in the entrepreneurial business, particularly on the gazelles, i.e., the businesses that grow quickly.

In economic theory, the entrepreneur is a capitalist owner, a pure risk taker whose reward is the profit, brings factors of production together and is crucial to economic development.

The entrepreneur according to economists:

- Intermediary – acts as a middleman
- Risk taker – profit reward for carrying risk
- Co-ordinator – links resources
- Creative and imaginative – able to think laterally
- Decision maker – able to make judgements
- Problem-solving – finds solutions
- Alert to profitable opportunities
- Identifies suppliers and customers
- Has special knowledge
- Makes a profit on the exchange
- An innovator – introduces new products or processes
- Catalyst for economic change
- No need to own resources

The development of entrepreneurship theories

The development of entrepreneurship theory can be traced back to some of the earliest writers about the economy. Some of the key writers on the topic include Cantillon, Schumpeter and Kirzner. Throughout the development of entrepreneurial theory, some of these have remained consistent. These include the entrepreneur as someone who can innovate and create jobs for themselves and for others. They are also willing to take risks for reward and can add value to organisations. The risk element, according to economists, is financial, i.e., the capital invested is risked in the new venture.

Cantillon

In economic theory, traditionally entrepreneurs were seen as capitalists who invested their own money and were rewarded accordingly. French economists distinguished between entrepreneurs and capitalists and saw entrepreneurs as risk takers. Cantillon (1755) was one of the first writers to introduce the concept of entrepreneurship. He defined entrepreneurs as those who did not have a fixed income. Entrepreneurs could, therefore, be separated from those with a fixed income, i.e., employees. He also described the entrepreneur as someone who could predict consumer demand. Cantillon identified the entrepreneur as someone who engages in market exchanges for profit. In this way they were different from the landowners and the employees who worked for a fixed income. The uncertainty faced by entrepreneurs is as a result of not knowing the final sale price. Traditionally, entrepreneurs were those who bought at one price and sold at another in the expectation of making a profit.

According to Cantillon, the entrepreneur was described by their behaviour and not their characteristics. He described the farmer as an entrepreneur who pays the landowner rent for the land without the certainty of knowing what the profit would be. The farmer cannot foresee which activity will pay best and must also contend with other factors, such as the weather, which can lead to uncertainty.

One of the interesting aspects about Cantillon's view of entrepreneurship was that he identified that anyone, regardless of their social status, could be an entrepreneur. Even today, entrepreneurship is seen as a way of increasing social mobility. He also pointed out that market forces would result in bankruptcy if there was too much competition. If there were too many hatters for the number of customers for the hats, then the entrepreneurs who didn't sell enough would go out of business. On the other hand, if there weren't enough hatters to meet the demand, then more hatters would be encouraged to set up in business and open more shops. If entrepreneurs fail to predict market demand, according to Cantillon, then they will face bankruptcy. Cantillon identified the entrepreneurs' decision-making in the face of uncertainty and this is one of his most important contribution to our understanding of entrepreneurship.

Schumpeter

Schumpeter (1934) identified creativity and innovation as an important element in entrepreneurship. According to Schumpeter, disequilibrium means that there is imperfect information. Entrepreneurs may have knowledge that is not available to anyone else. This could be based on gut instinct or identifying resources that are priced below their value and can be profitable if sold at a higher price, often by combining other resources. If other entrepreneurs also spot the same opportunity, then there will be increased competition and profits will be squeezed. Schumpeter said that entrepreneurship is about innovation, and that it was doing something different than the normal course of business. The entrepreneur brings the resources together to create new or better products or services. Schumpeter also wrote that the entrepreneur can also create a new market for these products. The innovations described by Schumpeter include the following:

• New product or an improvement in quality in an existing product
• New method of production, which does not need to be scientifically new

- New market where this market did not previously exist
- New source of materials
- New form of organisation in the industry, e.g., creation or breaking up of a monopoly

Schumpeter looked at the equilibrium approach to economic change and the concept that entrepreneurs were the catalyst for change because of their innovation. He described the economic equilibrium as a circular flow that happens routinely as the economy goes in waves from depression to economic growth and back again. The entrepreneur's role in this process is one of 'creative destruction' as they interrupt this circular flow. The entrepreneur brings in new processes of production and this interruption of the circular flow is what brings economic development,

The theoretical approach developed by Schumpeter was based on opposites, the interruption of the circular flow, change versus routine and also the difference between management and entrepreneurship. The function of management according to Schumpeter does not have the same economic impact because it is the entrepreneur who is dynamic and innovative. He saw management itself as static and that the entrepreneur can solve problems and do things in a way that hasn't been done previously.

Schumpeter described the entrepreneur as an agent of change, an innovator who introduces new products or processes. These changes were as a result of technological change and the entrepreneur develops new methods. In this way, the entrepreneur is a catalyst for economic change. Schumpeter also saw innovation in large firms who invest in research and development. Entrepreneurs are able to raise finance for their innovations when they can see rewards for their risks, and these interruptions to the cycle result in economic growth. Innovation in form of new products and services can give entrepreneurs a temporary monopoly, which gives them the resources needed to develop their business.

Kirzner

Kirzner (1973), an Austrian economist, said that entrepreneurship is about arbitrage, seizing opportunities and supplying resources lacking in the marketplace and this confirms the role of the entrepreneur as a middleman. Kirzner identified the entrepreneur as being 'alert' to opportunities for making a profit. He described this 'alertness' as being prepared to recognise opportunities and 'alertness to changed conditions or overlooked possibilities.' Kirzner's definition suggests that opportunities can be noticed even if people are not looking for them. It has been suggested that this alertness depends partly on some of the personal attributes of the individuals such as stamina, motivation and creativity. These personal attributes, such as tolerance of risk, ambiguity and uncertainty, can help entrepreneurs find new solutions to customers' needs and to develop new products or services that do not currently exist.

According to Kirzner, in the traditional economic approach of a market equilibrium where forces interact automatically, there is no room for individual decision-making. In reality, there is no perfect information and, therefore, markets are in disequilibrium and this is what provides opportunities for entrepreneurs. He was criticised for saying that the entrepreneur did not need their own capital. The entrepreneur will be alert to an opportunity and will seize it quickly. Kirzner gave the example of the arbitrageur, the person who buys at one price to sell at another price.

Uncertainty and risk

Successful entrepreneurs are able to tolerate high levels of risk, as they are willing to risk their own money as well as their reputation. They may also risk their home and their personal assets. Entrepreneurs do not see themselves as gamblers and they do calculate the risks carefully and do as much as possible to ensure that the venture succeeds. They will often share the risks with banks and other investors. Entrepreneurs try to limit the risk by sharing it with others. Creditors, customers and employees may also share the risks with the entrepreneur. Because entrepreneurs are often optimistic, they may consider the risks to be lower than those who are risk averse.

Entrepreneurs operate in an environment that is based on uncertainty and decision-making is often based on gut instinct. Uncertainty is in relation to income and information as well as other aspects of their business. Entrepreneurs face uncertainty in that they do not have a guaranteed income and they have to generate sufficient sales to pay the costs of running the business. This can cause higher levels of uncertainty and risk if the entrepreneur has personal assets at risk.

A small market share may mean that entrepreneurs are in a poor negotiating position with regard to prices. Many small firms, for example, are reliant on large firms as subcontractors and are unable to get the best prices for their goods and services. They may also be in a weak position with regard to buying goods and services. The entrepreneur may not be maximising profits or sales but a level of income, or survival of the business. Another source of uncertainty is the amount of change taking place in a new business. They will go through a number of changes as they grow, which will influence how the entrepreneur manages the business as well as the management structure as the business grows.

Innovation and creativity

The entrepreneur is traditionally seen as an innovator (Schumpeter, 1934) and they can also implement their ideas. They will often learn by trial and error and learn from their mistakes, e.g., James Dyson, who built thousands of prototypes for his bagless vacuum cleaner. High levels of risk combined with low levels of resources require the entrepreneur to have high levels of creativity. A new venture will have a very simple organisational form, with the entrepreneur initially managing all aspects of the business. Low levels of resources means that the entrepreneur has to be creative with all aspects of the business, especially developing and marketing the new product or service.

The trait and behavioural approach to entrepreneurship

The theories of entrepreneurship can be divided into two main approaches (Figure 2.1). The first approach looks at entrepreneurial traits, i.e., what are the characteristics of the entrepreneurs? What differentiates them from other people? The second approach is asking what do entrepreneurs do? The theories regarding entrepreneurship can be divided into two approaches; the first one looks at what the entrepreneur does, e.g., creates a new venture, and secondly, what are the character traits of the entrepreneurs and can a 'type' of person be identified who is entrepreneurial (Table 2.1)?

The question of why some people start a business has focused on the character traits of the entrepreneurs. Some of the theories that have been prevalent in the theories about entrepreneurship include the need for achievement and their attitudes towards risk. The trait approach attempts to find out what is different about entrepreneurs that can identify those most likely to start a business. Entrepreneurs who have failed with one business often go on to start successful other businesses. This would imply that entrepreneurial skills can be learned rather than inherent in the individual. Entrepreneurs will face many problems in setting up a new business. Some of these skills

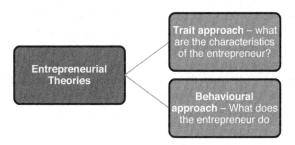

Figure 2.1 Entrepreneurial theories

Table 2.1 The trait and behavioural approach to entrepreneurship

Trait approach	Behavioural approach
What are the characteristics of the entrepreneur?	*What does the entrepreneur do?*
Need for achievement	Perceives opportunities
High locus of control	Creates solutions
Independent	Takes reasonable risks
Energetic	Builds something of value
Wants to succeed	Starts business
Able to make decisions	Raises finance
Leaders	Develops new projects
Creative and innovative	Organises and manages the business on a day to day business

that could be learned from failure would be the identification of which problems need urgent attention.

It is clear that entrepreneurs need many different skills as they set up a new business. They will go through a learning curve that will include management of all aspects, including financial, operations, people and other resources. However, one of the most important aspects will be building a team to help run the business.

Entrepreneurs and management

The 19th-century economists distinguished between entrepreneurs and managers in that the entrepreneurs were bearing the financial risk. In the 19th century, entrepreneurship was limited to those with wealth. An important development was the separation of ownership and management following the Joint Stock Act. This also paved the way for shares to be sold to the public and money could be raised in this way for new or existing businesses.

By the mid-20th century, *entrepreneurship* was used not only to describe the risk-bearing innovative individuals but also those who manage a business enterprise. In economic theory, the entrepreneur responds to market forces and will enter the market when there is disequilibrium, i.e., prices exceed costs and there is potential for profits. It is then assumed that profit maximisation is the sole objective. However, this contrasts with surveys of entrepreneurs who state that making profits is only one of their motivations for starting a business.

Capital

The amount of capital required depends on the industry. Many entrepreneurs start businesses where the barriers to entry are low. However, low barriers to entry mean that other entrepreneurs can also enter this market and this will increase pressure on prices and make it more difficult for the new venture to survive. Entrepreneurs often start businesses in the industry where they have experience, but if the capital requirements are very high, then they are less likely to start a new business.

The negative side of entrepreneurship

De Vries (1977) saw entrepreneurs as displaced and dissatisfied people who would find it difficult to work in a structured environment. Entrepreneurship may be in preference to employment, especially in a large firm, for those unable to deal with being told what to do.

Case study: Uber

Travis Kalanik is the entrepreneur who co-founded Uber, the taxi-hailing company, UberEats and other Uber businesses. Uber had flouted many laws in cities in the US to become established, including permits and other violations. Kalanik believed that he was shaking up an industry that was expensive and inefficient and once people tried his system of calling a cab, they would use it. Uber became one of the fastest growing companies, with its service available in cities all over the world.

Known for his flamboyant lifestyle and lavish parties for staff, including singers such as Beyoncé to entertain them, Kalanik was able to preside over the rapid growth and achieve acceptance of Uber as a transport alternative. As a child, he was able to do arithmetical calculations in his head and he went on to study economics and computer science at UCLA. His first venture was Scour.net, which gave users the ability to search for and download files, including films and music. Kalanik would focus on his business to the exclusion of everything else, but it went out of business.

The idea for Uber was initially developed by Garrett Camp, who was inspired by a James Bond film and the iPhone technology. He got together with Kalanik and drivers were given iPhones, which had been bought in bulk at discounted prices. The company, which was called UberCab, was facing prosecution for breaking transportation laws. Kalanik decided to ignore the threat of prosecution and changed the name of the business to Uber.

Uber gave out free rides to attract customers and also paid out bonuses to drivers and growth was rapid in all the cities where it was available. Checking the drivers was outsourced to a company that could provide a quick turn-around. The drivers were described as contract workers and, therefore, were not employed by Uber, which meant that the company was not liable for holiday pay, insurance and other benefits.

At the same time that Uber was growing quickly, Kalanik himself became increasingly unpopular. He was living the high life whilst at the same time the drivers were getting low wages and traditional taxi drivers were losing their livelihood. His focus on the numbers and growth was at the detriment of the employees' and the drivers' welfare. By 2017, the senior managers were concerned about Kalanik's negative image and a video showing his lack of concern for his drivers was circulated. He was forced to resign as CEO but still retains a large shareholding in Uber.

Discussion

1   How did Kalanik's attitude towards disrupting the industry affect Uber's growth?
2   Why is it important for entrepreneurs to treat their employees with respect?

Exercise

•   Identify other examples of the gig or sharing economy.

Family entrepreneurship

Families are an important influence on entrepreneurship. Ninety percent of the businesses in the UK are family businesses and many of these are run by husband-and-wife teams. The GEM report 2018/19 found that one in five entrepreneurs in the 47 countries surveyed will be starting a business with family members. Family background is considered an important influence on entrepreneurs and children growing up in an entrepreneurial family are more likely to start a business themselves.

Some entrepreneurs inherit the family business as it is passed down from generation to generation. There are many examples of successful family businesses in the UK and in other countries, such as Clarks Shoes and JCB. Family businesses are usually started by one or two entrepreneurs and then, as it becomes bigger, they will be joined by others. What is a family business? A business is generally considered a family business if more than one family member is working in the business, the family control the equity and the business is passed down to the next generation.

There are fundamental differences between family- and non-family-controlled businesses. These differences include the following:

•   Long-term approach to strategy and planning
•   Higher risk aversion than in non-family businesses
•   Decision making in the hands of key family members
•   Family culture

Some family members may not work full-time in the business and will only help out when necessary. They may be more flexible than other staff members and may not seek financial recompense. One of the main advantages of a family business is the trust between family members, although this is not necessarily the case, as these are examples where family members have fallen out and this can cause problems. In Germany, Karl and Theo Albrecht took over their mother's grocery shop and built Aldi into a successful retailer. However, the two brothers fell out over whether to sell cigarettes and the company was split into two.

The priorities and the management in a family business are likely to be different in that the entrepreneurs will take a long-term approach with a view to passing the business to the next generation. Although the perception of family business is that they are small scale serving local markets, there are many examples of large multinational companies, such as Estée Lauder and JCB. Some of the other well-known family businesses include Walmart in the US, Tata in India and BMW in Germany.

One of the key elements in a family business is how to transfer management to the next generation. The transfer of assets and management to the next generation can be difficult and only a small percentage of family firms survive to the third generation.

Family firms often have lower cost structures and are also very careful when it comes to capital expenditure. They tend to invest only in very strong projects. This means that they may miss some good opportunities but, as a result, they will have reduced their exposure to risks. Family firms often have a lower level of debt than nonfamily firms. They also avoid acquisitions and prefer organic growth. They are also more diversified than nonfamily businesses and this can also reduce the level of risk. Family firms are often more export-focused and willing to invest in developing international markets. They are also better at retaining staff and this is achieved by treating them as family and avoiding redundancies. The family culture is an integral part of the family business. Successful family firms such as Cadburys were originally built around strong ethics and values that were shared with the workforce. The entrepreneurial culture and values, such as looking after employees, can also be passed down from generation to generation.

Social entrepreneurship

What is a social enterprise? A social enterprise is usually a not-for-profit enterprise that is intended to help the community. These enterprises can take many forms. Social entrepreneurship covers a wide variety of activities including community shops, banks and other organisations to help the community. The definition of a social enterprise used by the UK government is 'a business with primarily social objectives whose surpluses are principally reinvested for that purpose in the business or in the community, rather than being driven by the need to maximize profit for shareholders and owners' (BIS, 2011:2).

A social enterprise can take many forms: a co-operative, a housing association, a charity or a non-governmental organisation (NGO). Many social enterprises, large and small, are companies limited by guarantee, including clubs and political parties. There are no shareholders but the directors must provide a nominal guarantee. Under the 2004 Companies Act, the community interest company was introduced to allow companies to reinvest their surplus for the benefit of the community. Other legal forms include the industrial and provident societies, which include co-operative societies and community benefit societies. A limited liability partnership can also be used for social enterprises.

Although the concept of entrepreneurship is closely linked to making a profit, the other dimension is the identification of an opportunity or a problem than needs to be solved. The other aspect of entrepreneurship that is relevant to the not-for-profit sector is the ability to make fundamental changes.

The social enterprise depends on a variety of factors for success, including fundraising from various charities and donations, as well as grants and loans. They also depend on an effective management team and support from volunteers, who often give their time without pay. Often, the motivation for the social enterprise will be a gap in the private or public sector. Although making a profit may not be a primary consideration, nevertheless the survival of the social enterprise will depend on ensuring sufficient income to cover the running costs.

Rural entrepreneurship

Entrepreneurial activities in rural areas are described as rural entrepreneurship. Some of these activities can only take place in their location because of specific natural resources. These can include food and drink with a Protected Designation of Origin status awarded by the EU, e.g., Halen Môn (Anglesey Sea Salt). Rural areas are characterised by low population and distance from the markets leading to poor demand and, consequently, low levels of economic activity. There is also a high dependence on agriculture and tourism, which can be seasonal, as well as poor access to finance and infrastructure such as fast broadband, which can limit growth. Diversification in agriculture is seen as a key factor in rural entrepreneurship. Entrepreneurs in rural areas may be motivated by wanting to maintain or improve their quality of life and the social and cultural elements may be very important to them and, therefore, they will adopt strategies that enable them to stay in that location. The utilisation of local resources may give them a competitive advantage.

References

BIS (2011). A guide to legal forms for social enterprise. *Department for Business Innovation and Skills*. Retrieved October 11, 2019, from https://assets. publishing.service.gov.uk/government/uploads/system/uploads/attachment_data/ file/31677/11-1400-guide-legal-forms-for-social-enterprise.pdf

Bosma, N., & Kelley, D. (2019). *Global Entrepreneurship monitor 2018/2019 global report*. Babson Park: Global Entrepreneurship Research Association.

Cantillon, R. (1755). *Essay on the nature of general commerce*. Henry Higgs, trans. London: Macmllan.

De Vries, M. K. (1977). The entrepreneurial personality: A person at the crossroads. *Journal of Management Studies, 14*(1), 34–57.

Hébert, R. F., & Link, A. N. (1989). In search of the meaning of entrepreneurship. *Small Business Economics, 1*(1), 39–49.

Kirzner, I. M. (1973). *Competition and entrepreneurship*. Chicago: University of Chicago Press.

Schumpeter, J. A. (1934). *The theory of economic development*. Cambridge, MA: Harvard University Press.

3 The entrepreneur, characteristics and personality

Summary

One of the first writers to describe the entrepreneur was Jean-Baptise Say. He described the entrepreneur as a person who could forecast demand and create value. There has been considerable work on the personality traits including the psychodynamic model, which portrays the entrepreneur as a rebel. Characteristics of the entrepreneur include their desire to be independent, work hard and usually have good communication skills. They are also able to raise finance, can make decisions and are motivated to succeed. Entrepreneurs are motivated by social and environmental factors and some may be 'pushed' into entrepreneurship in order to create an income. Others may decide to start a business because they have identified an opportunity. One of the functions of the entrepreneur is to develop new products and services as well as new markets and technology. Lifestyle entrepreneurs want the business to provide them with an income, whereas others want to grow and expand. Some technology entrepreneurs have become billionaires in a very short time and they have transformed the way people live and work. The gig and sharing economy is based on online platforms that have become very successful. Intrapreneurs are those who have an entrepreneurial approach in a large organisation. A growing sector is the senior entrepreneurs who start a business later on in life.

Introduction

Today, the concept of the 'entrepreneur' is quite wide. However, there is general consensus about what an entrepreneur does, i.e., set up a new business. The entrepreneur can spot opportunities and they can come up with solutions to problems. They can also organise the resources to provide these solutions and create wealth in the process. As we can see with examples such as Amazon, making a profit isn't always necessary, as entrepreneurs have become wealthy by creating businesses that have attracted investors and have turnover. Entrepreneurs can also accept the risk of failure and change direction or start again when one business fails.

Entrepreneurs are all different and there is no one single psychological profile. Successful entrepreneurs are enthusiastic, willing to work hard and have a positive attitude towards risk. Entrepreneurs are influenced by a number of factors, including their family, education, role models, society, etc. They are highly motivated and able to learn quickly to bring together the resources needed to start a business. Most successful entrepreneurs have a vision or a long-term strategy for their business and are able to communicate this to both customers and providers of external finance.

The term *entrepreneur'* was first used by Say (1836) and, although it may have been around previously, he was the first to describe the functions. Say described situations where land, capital and an industry (hard work) did not need to be held by one person and could be transferred, e.g., the landowner could lend his estate to someone who had capital and industry in exchange for rent. One of the first examples of an entrepreneur is given by Say (1836:45):

> The knife-grinder's craft requires no occupancy of land; he carries his stock in trade upon his shoulders, and his skill and industry at his fingers' ends; being at the same time an entrepreneur, capitalist and labourer.

Many attempts have been made to translate the word *entrepreneur* into other languages. One suggestion for an English translation is 'undertaker,' but that is normally used for another purpose. Another suggestion by one of the translators of Say's work is 'adventurer' and, again, this has another meaning. The French word *entrepreneur* is, therefore, the one in common usage to describe someone who creates their own income. Say also described the entrepreneur as a manager who could forecast demand. Say was one of the first writers to link entrepreneurship to the economy. He saw entrepreneurs as intermediaries, who bring resources together to meet customer demand. Entrepreneurs, according to Say, are central to the production process as they bring together the knowledge and the application of the entrepreneur. He also saw entrepreneurs as those who could predict market demand.

Definitions of the entrepreneur

There is no agreed definition of the entrepreneur. The economists' view of the entrepreneur is as a capitalist and risk-taker who brings together the factors of production for profit. The word *entreprendre* literally translated means 'take between,' and portrays the entrepreneur in the role of the middleman. Attempts have been made to translate it into English and other languages, although it is a difficult concept to convey in any language.

Say (1836) defined the entrepreneur as the person who brings together the factors of production and creates value in the products. The entrepreneur invests capital, pays wages and rent and then makes a profit. In order to do this, the entrepreneur has to have some personal qualities including 'judgment, perseverance and knowledge of the world of business (Say, 1835:45).'

The economists' view of the entrepreneur is as capitalists who invest in their own business for profit. The profit is seen as a reward for their investment. However, later economists distinguished between entrepreneurs and capitalists. Say (1836) also saw the entrepreneur as someone who could forecast demand. Many definitions look at what the entrepreneur does. The major functions of the entrepreneur, according to economists, are the bearing of risk and uncertainty and the organisation and management of a business enterprise.

Personality and character traits of entrepreneurs

Traditionally, there has been a common belief that entrepreneurs are 'born and not made' and that successful entrepreneurs have innate abilities such as being proactive and achievement oriented. They do have a need for independence and autonomy and a high internal locus of control, which means they want to be in control of their environment. They often have a long-term approach and a vision both for themselves and their business. They are also self-confident and there are many examples of their ability to deal with failure and start again. However, one of the main criticisms of this approach is that these characteristics may also apply to other people including senior managers. This approach also ignores external factors, such as education and role models, which have influenced them.

Chell (1985) looked at the entrepreneurial personality and identified three psychological approaches: the psychodynamic model, the social development model and the trait approach. The psychodynamic model portrays the entrepreneurial personality as having a troubled background, which has led to issues with self-esteem and the need to be in control. The entrepreneur is then seen as a rebel who then finds it difficult to conform. Consequently, entrepreneurs then start their own business as they would find it difficult to fit in with large organisations. However, there are criticisms of this approach that describes the entrepreneur as a deviant personality, as it may apply to only a small percentage.

However, there are some elements that may be relevant to this theory. The first one is that inertia may be an important factor in that people who are happy in their jobs may not leave to start a new business. The second one is the 'pull' effect of wanting a higher status in society. Thirdly, there may also be the 'push' effect of not wanting to work for someone else or feeling underpaid and with very little opportunity for promotion.

The social development model assumes that entrepreneurs are influenced by their environment, rather than having inherent entrepreneurial traits. People are influenced by different factors at each stage of their lives and there may be different events and pressures at each stage, which motivate entrepreneurs. This approach has been criticised, as it difficult to assign behaviour purely to social and environmental influences.

The most popular approach to entrepreneurship has been the trait model. The aim of the trait model is to differentiate entrepreneurs from people who do not start a business. There is consensus that some traits can be identified, such as the need for achievement, persistence and self-confidence. One of the problems with this approach is that successful entrepreneurs may develop traits after they have started a business. Persistence may be necessary as the entrepreneur doesn't want to fail and self-confidence may develop as the business grows due to external validation. This approach has been criticised because some of the traits can also be observed in senior managers. The other issues include whether entrepreneurs can learn entrepreneurial skills and also how they react to different events and situations.

Characteristics of the entrepreneur

Although it is difficult to generalise about the characteristics of the entrepreneur, there is consensus about some of them. Entrepreneurs are committed and determined and are willing to work hard. They can identify an opportunity and have knowledge of market needs and how to address them. Although entrepreneurs are often described as willing to take risks, these are calculated risks. They are also able to solve problems and may be nonconventional and able to think laterally. Because of the changing needs of the business and the market, entrepreneurs have to be adaptable and willing to change. They also have to be creative and innovative and driven to succeed.

Characteristics of the entrepreneur include the following:

- Creative and innovative
- Drives economic change
- Determined and driven
- Desire to be independent
- Willing to take calculated risks

- Flexible and willing to work hard
- Good communication skills
- Proactive
- Wants to be in control
- Need for achievement
- Develops networks
- Independent
- Motivated to succeed
- Able to forecast demand
- Takes responsibility
- Makes decisions under uncertainty

Personal attributes

Some of the personal attributes of the entrepreneurs include energy and stamina as they need to be able to work long hours, especially in the early stages of the business. They are also committed and dedicated and motivated to succeed. They are often all-rounders and have a wide variety of skills or are prepared to learn. They are able to assess the opportunities and can tolerate the risks associated with starting and growing a business. Successful entrepreneurs are competitive and also have a sense of urgency and the need to get things done. They also feel a sense of responsibility, especially for their employees. They are often driven to succeed and are dedicated to achieving their vision for the business.

Entrepreneurs may have personal attributes such as creativity and the ability to network. They may also be able to focus on their objectives for themselves and their business. Entrepreneurs are often described as courageous, possibly because of their willingness to take risks and follow their gut instinct to start a business. They are often able to assess the competition and find their strengths and weaknesses in order to find a gap in the market. Entrepreneurs can make things happen, and often feel the urgency to get things done quickly. They are often dedicated to building their business and put in long hours and often learn, not only from experience, but also from their mistakes.

Entrepreneurs often use bootstrapping techniques to start a business with very little or no money. They are able to motivate family and friends in the early stages to give them support. As the business grows, entrepreneurs are willing and able to raise external finance from other sources, including banks and investors. If they want to raise equity finance, this means giving up part of their business and this may be difficult for some entrepreneurs. However, this does mean that they share the risks with other people and building a good team is essential for their success.

Personal characteristics

Decision making

Entrepreneurs are able to make quick decisions. This can give the smaller businesses an advantage over larger ones, as they can move more quickly. Many entrepreneurs are confident in their own ability to make decisions, although overconfidence can also cause problems.

Able to sell

One of the key skills that an entrepreneur needs is to be able to sell their products or services. Raising money and getting customers, especially in the early stages, need good selling skills. Being able to convince banks and other investors of the idea is also important. Entrepreneurs may develop selling skills. However, it is often their enthusiasm and belief in the product or service that enables them to get started.

Want to succeed

Many entrepreneurs may be motivated to succeed and this acts as an impetus for them to start their own business. This motivation may be as a result is seeing the rewards that their role models have achieved such as the nice house and car.

High energy

In order to succeed in business, entrepreneurs may have to work very hard and put in a lot of extra hours, especially in the early stages. This means that they have to have lots of energy so that they can keep going for long hours. They also have to lead by example if they are employing other people and may often start early and finish later than their employees.

Social and environmental factors

The motivations to become an entrepreneur and start a new venture can depend on many different factors. However, these can be divided into two types: 'push' and 'pull' (Figure 3.1).

Some entrepreneurs start a business because they cannot find a suitable job, or they may have moved into a new area where there are few alternatives. The others decide to start a business because they have spotted an opportunity or they want a better income.

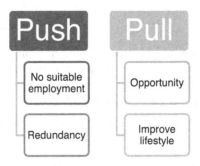

Figure 3.1 Push and pull factors for entrepreneurship

Social factors can also have an impact on entrepreneurship. The most popular age to start a business is 35–54. The GEM report (Bosma and Kelley, 2019) found that the most prevalent age for starting a business was in either 25–34 or the 35–44 age ranges. It is possible that, in these age ranges, entrepreneurs have had the opportunity to explore opportunities and also to build up assets in the form of savings or equity.

There is also some evidence to indicate that entrepreneurship runs in families and those whose parents ran their own business are more likely to emulate them. Entrepreneurship is also more prevalent in married couples than singles and this may be because of the emotional and financial support given by a spouse. Some entrepreneurs are motivated by marginalisation, for example, some ethnic groups and immigrants are more likely to become entrepreneurs.

Environmental factors such as the industrial structure in an area can influence entrepreneurship. Clusters of technically advanced businesses can provide support for each other and the exchange of knowledge encourages innovation. One example of this is Silicon Valley in California where high technology businesses are able to exchange ideas and also provide opportunities for staff to move from one business to another. Other factors include the availability of finance from banks and financial institutions and Sequoia Capital is an example having made investments in Yahoo!, Google and Airbnb. An affluent population also provide more opportunities for entrepreneurs to succeed and rising house prices can also help to provide available equity to finance a new business.

Experience and knowledge

Much has been written about the specialist knowledge that entrepreneurs have. Many entrepreneurs start a business in the same field that they have been working in. They may even start a business in competition with their previous employer. This may be because of the different kinds of experience and knowledge available but also because small firms may have lower barriers to entry and it may be easier to set up in competition. They also have knowledge and access to the best customers.

Education

In the UK, traditionally, entrepreneurs have very few educational qualifications although that situation is gradually changing. Famous entrepreneurs such as Alan Sugar and Richard Branson left school without any formal qualifications. Entrepreneurs in some sectors are more likely to be better educated, for example, those starting a business in science or technology. There are also some sectors where entrepreneurs are less likely to be educated to a higher level, such as the self-employed in the construction sector.

One of the benefits of education is the greater choice of jobs and of career opportunities. The entrepreneur from the middle or upper class is likely to be better educated and be wealthier. In the technological and biotechnology industries in particular, there is a need to be well qualified before obtaining employment. Education should theoretically improve the performance and management of a new venture. One of the concerns in the UK has been the low participation in science and technology education and that this would have an adverse effect on innovation. Some minority groups who are better educated, such as immigrants, may decide to start a business rather than look for a job.

Case study: Jose Neves

Jose Neves grew up in Porto in Portugal and developed the website Farfetch. Farfetch sells designer clothes, shoes and accessories from designers such as Gucci, Fendi, Burberry, Stella McCartney and Prada. The company was valued at $9 billion following the launch on the New York Stock Exchange in 2018 and Neves became a billionaire after the initial public offering (IPO). Despite this, the company has not yet made a profit and the share price dropped almost 40% in the year after the launch following higher than expected losses. He always had a belief that the company was going to succeed and he had sold part of the business for nearly $400 million in 2017 in order to expand to China.

Neves studied economics at university in Portugal and his ambition was to move to London. The area where he grew up had lots of clothes and shoe manufacturers. He was very interested in computer programming and started helping his relatives who owned shoe shops to manage their production. When he was 21, he thought he could do anything, even design shoes. He got married and moved to London to set up a shoe shop. He then opened up a shop selling up-and-coming designers. He saw the success of Asos and Net-a-Porter and thought he could set up an online business selling the products of the best independent retailers. He spent a year developing Farfetch and then launched in 2008 at the start of the credit crunch and this led to very tough time. However, the credit crunch also helped sales because the luxury retailers were looking for sales and were willing to sell through the Farfetch website. Following the credit crunch, investors were looking for opportunities and were keen to invest in Farfetch.

For discussion

1   How important was it that Neves thought that the business would be successful? Did this help him raise external finance?
2   Neves thought he could do anything. Is this typical of an entrepreneur?

Exercise

•   Identify a group of products that you could sell from one website such as Farfetch.

Role and function of the entrepreneur

One of the aspects that differentiates successful entrepreneurs is that if they spot an opportunity, then can act on it and bring the resources together to make it work. As they can act relatively quickly to get a new venture off the ground, they may also have a first-mover advantage in the market.

A new opportunity does not have to be a brand new product. It can be in the form of an extension to an existing market or developing a new market for an existing product or services. A new market can be created either for a new or an existing product or service. There are some entrepreneurs that have created an entirely new market by developing a product or service that didn't exist before. However, the majority of new products or services are changes to existing ones.

There is a general consensus that the entrepreneur is the person who starts a new venture and develops new products and services (Figure 3.2). However, in order to start a new business, the entrepreneur must first spot an opportunity and create a solution to a problem. For example, Airbnb was started when the founders, Brian Chesky and Joe Gebbia, put an air mattress on their floor in order to raise money when they were struggling to pay the rent on their apartment. They managed to raise seed money from Sequoia capital and developed their business.

Figure 3.2 Role and function of the entrepreneur

What does the entrepreneur do?

- Takes reasonable risks
- Builds something of value
- Takes responsibility for the risks
- Sorts out problems
- Can forecast demand
- Makes a profit (or loss)
- Develops a new product or service

New product

Although the majority of new products are actually refinements of an existing product or service, there are some that are completely new. The Sinclair C5, for example, was one of the first electric cars. Although it was not a commercial success, it was the forerunner of the electric cars we see today.

New market

Some entrepreneurs can find a new market for an existing product or service. Sometimes this can be as a result of low sales for the existing product or service and the entrepreneur then has to find alternatives or go out of business. Or the entrepreneur can spot an opportunity for a new market for an existing product or service.

New development

One of the ways that entrepreneurs can add value to existing products or services is by new development.

New technology

An example of this is the Dyson vacuum cleaner. The product, i.e., the vacuum cleaner, was already in existence and Dyson developed the bagless technology.

Resources

The entrepreneur can bring together the resources required to start a new business. These resources can include the following:

- Finance
- Assets – equipment – premises
- People
- Other support – accountants – solicitors – enterprise agencies

The entrepreneur has to play different roles in the business, especially in the early stages. When Laura Tenison of JoJo Maman Bebe started her business, she had a wheelie chair and a long desk with different phones so that she could answer each query in a different role. The roles included chief executive, sales manager, purchaser, production manager, accounts payable and answering any other queries from customers and suppliers. Some entrepreneurs will clean their premises after the staff members have gone home.

The problem with this approach is that the entrepreneur will have to decide whether to take on staff or keep the business small enough that they can perform most of the tasks. Delegation is a skill that must be learnt and this is difficult especially if the people employed are not as competent as the entrepreneur. This can lead to frustration and the key is to select employees carefully. However, many entrepreneurs will employ friends and family in the first instance or people who ask for a job and they may not have the necessary skills. Customers of small businesses also often want to deal with the owner and this relationship is an important one, as it brings in sales. The entrepreneur may also enjoy developing these relationships as they increase their feeling of worth and self-confidence. In addition, the entrepreneur will want to make sure these customers are happy so that they can make word of mouth recommendations.

People who work in part-time or even full-time jobs without paying taxes are what's known as the 'black economy.' This is because they are not registered as a business or as self-employed and don't pay taxes on their earnings. They usually work for cash and can work in any industry, although they are more prevalent in some industries than others. Governments want to legitimise the workers in the black economy and encourage those people to become self-employed.

In North America, technology entrepreneurs have transformed the way we live and work. In the UK and Europe, and in other countries, there are examples of entrepreneurs, such as Richard Branson and Anita Roddick, who have been used as role models. Roddick founded the Body Shop and transformed the way we look at politics and animal testing and used her shops to promote environmental issues. Up until Bill Gates established Microsoft in the 1970s, the computer industry in North America was dominated by large firms such as IBM. Yet IBM was to face serious problems, whereas young entrepreneurial businesses such as Apple, Dell and Microsoft went from strength to strength.

Case study: Richard Branson

Richard Branson is one of the UK's best known entrepreneurs. He left school with no formal educational qualifications because of his dyslexia and he started his first business with very few resources. His first business was a student magazine and he subsequently set up Virgin Records. The business was struggling until Mike Oldfield recorded *Tubular Bells* and became a best seller. Since then, Branson has used the Virgin brand to promote different types of businesses including Virgin Atlantic and Virgin trains.

By the early 1990s, the Virgin empire was facing cash-flow problems and Richard Branson had to sell Virgin Records to EMI in order to put the money into Virgin Atlantic. Other brands include Virgin Media and Virgin Money. One of his most recent ventures is Virgin Galactic, which will take tourists into space, although an accident in 2014 delayed this venture. Branson has always been willing to use his high profile, including by dressing up in a wedding dress, to promote his businesses and to take risks, both financial and physical. His exploits include attempts to circumnavigate the world by hot air balloon and crossing the Atlantic in a speedboat.

For discussion

1   Identify some of the characteristics of Richard Branson that you would describe as entrepreneurial.
2   How has Richard Branson established such as successful brand?

Exercise

- What type of businesses use the Virgin brand and how can this concept be expanded to other areas?

Types of entrepreneurs

Potential entrepreneurs

Potential entrepreneurs are those who are planning to start a business in the future.

Nascent entrepreneurs

Nascent entrepreneurs are those who are in the process of setting up the business but have not yet started trading. They have not yet started taking an income from the business.

Hobby entrepreneurs

The entrepreneur has a full-time job and a hobby that brings in additional income, e.g., bee-keeping. This may provide the basis for giving up employment to work in the business full-time.

Lifestyle and growth entrepreneurs

Some entrepreneurs want to grow their business quickly and are willing to employ more people and raise finance, if necessary for expansion (Table 3.1). Other entrepreneurs are happy to stay small and have a business that they can manage themselves and that provides them with a comfortable living. These are called 'lifestyle entrepreneurs.' Their business may not stay small from choice and they may be unable to grow their business for a number of reasons including insufficient sales.

Some lifestyle entrepreneurs prefer to trade off income for flexible hours and more control over their activities. There are some lifestyle entrepreneurs who have started a business and see it grow very quickly and become a

Table 3.1 Stages of growth

Existence	Business is established
Survival	The entrepreneur manages to keep the business going
Success	The business is profitable and relatively stable
Take-off	Profits increase and the business expands
Maturity	Profits stabilise and growth slows down

success. However, despite the growth potential of the business, it could still be constrained by the aspirations of the entrepreneur.

Technology entrepreneurs

- Bill Gates – Microsoft
- Michael Dell – Dell Computers
- Steve Jobs – Apple Computers

These entrepreneurs started their businesses while they were in their 20s and they have transformed people's lives, including their own, their employees and their investors. There are many others who started at a relatively young age. Some of these firms, such as Apple, eBay and Yahoo!, have had venture capital investment, which has helped them become household names.

The internet has transformed the way businesses work and has provided technology entrepreneurs with the way of starting and growing a business very rapidly. We have seen how some internet entrepreneurs have transformed the way we live and work. These entrepreneurs became billionaires in a very short amount of time.

The internet has created the world's youngest billionaire entrepreneurs in the shortest time (Table 3.2); Sergei Brin and Larry Page set up Google in the 1990s and went from students to billionaires in five years. Mark Zuckerberg, who founded Facebook, became a billionaire in his 20s. Jeff Bezos founded Amazon in his garage in Seattle. Pierre Omidyar founded eBay and became a billionaire by age 31. Many of these firms were funded by Sequoia Capital. Some of these firms took years to make a profit, if any, yet they became household names.

Some of these entrepreneurs did not develop the initial product themselves. Bill Gates, who is one of the richest billionaires in the world, launched Microsoft when he was 19 years old with his partner, Paul Allen, in 1975. In 1979, IBM chose Microsoft to run its operating system and they purchased an operating system from another company and renamed

Table 3.2 Technology entrepreneurs

Larry Page and Sergei Brin	Google
Jeff Bezos	Amazon
Mark Zuckerberg	Facebook
Jerry Yang, David Filo	Yahoo!
Elon Musk	PayPal
Bill Gates, Paul Allen	Microsoft

it MS-DOS. This was a great success as the market for personal computers took off and the software was sold with each machine.

Portfolio entrepreneurs

Portfolio entrepreneurs are those who have several businesses running at the same time. These businesses may be a diversification of the existing business or a completely different business.

Serial entrepreneurs

Serial entrepreneurs have started one business and then moved on to another. Some entrepreneurs enjoy starting new businesses and either sell them or step back once they are established. They may also be described as habitual entrepreneurs. Easyjet was floated on the stock exchange in 2000 and Stelios Haji-Ioannou decided to step down as chief executive and then chairman. This gave him the opportunity to create other businesses and he started selling some of his shares in Easyjet to finance new ventures, including Easycar, Easymoney and Easycinema. Stelios describes himself as a serial entrepreneur and that he is always looking for another idea.

Solo entrepreneurs

Solo entrepreneurs are running their business on their own with no employees.

Gig entrepreneurs and the sharing economy

The increasing online platforms such as Uber, Airbnb and Etsy have brought opportunities for entrepreneurs who can work full- or part-time. These popular online platforms can provide opportunities for people to have a sideline or a more substantial income. For example, entrepreneurs in the sharing economy could be getting income from sharing part of their home or other assets. Gig entrepreneurs can also find temporary work online. It is possible that starting with a temporary gig or participating in the sharing economy may lead to the development of future entrepreneurial opportunities. However, there are also concerns that the gig and the sharing economies are undercutting existing businesses.

Franchise entrepreneurs

Franchising is an increasingly important part of the economy and entrepreneurship. The original entrepreneur develops an innovation in retail or services and then franchises the idea. Franchising is essentially the replication of the business in another location. Franchising works by charging a royalty for the use of a brand and other fees such as training and marketing. The franchise agreement will cover a specific area and will be for a period of time. Usually, the franchise can have the exclusive right to sell the product or service in a specified area, although there are also nonexclusive agreements. By starting a business as a franchisee, the entrepreneur is reducing the risk in that they are buying the right to use a proven business model and a reduced failure rate. There is also support available from the franchisor as well as training for both the entrepreneur and the staff.

Both the franchisor and the franchise have obligations to each other. The franchisor has to protect the brand and the business concept. The franchisee has to provide goods and services in accordance with the business model developed by the franchisor. The way that this is done is through standardisation and the service delivery system. The premises have to display the logo and all the decor has to be in accordance with company policy. Staff usually have to wear uniforms in the colour and style of the franchisor. Some of aspects of the relationship may cause problems, especially if the franchisee wants to be innovative or the franchisor is not marketing the product or service adequately.

Intrapreneurs

Intrapreneurs are people who are considered entrepreneurial in large organisations and in the public sector. There is a consensus that entrepreneurship is found not only in small businesses but also in large organisations and in the public sector. Many large organisations have relatively bureaucratic structures and processes and this can limit innovation and creativity. Intrapreneurs can stimulate and lead change by creating new ideas and implementing them. There are different roles that the intrapreneur can adopt, including being an innovator and developing new products, services and markets. They can also act as a product champion, organising the resources necessary to bring a new concept to market. The third role is overcoming obstacles and objections to new developments, and, fourthly, they can commercialise an existing idea.

Senior entrepreneurs

There are an increasing number of people over 65 years who are active and healthy, and this is one of the fastest growing groups of entrepreneurs. There are many examples of successful entrepreneurs who have started their business later in life. Ray Krok, who founded McDonald's, started his business at 54 years old. He brought a wealth of knowledge and experience to the business and was able to grow it rapidly using the franchise model.

Schøtt et al. (2017) noted that older people have lower levels of entrepreneurial intentions. However, entrepreneurial intentions amongst the elderly are linked to income levels with those with a higher income more likely to have entrepreneurial intentions. Becoming unemployed is one of the main motivations for starting a business, although there is a sharp decline in the number of people starting a business after 50 years of age. They may also be more likely to become social entrepreneurs than younger people. Senior entrepreneurs are more likely to fund the business from their own funds, possibly as a result of receiving redundancy payments.

In some countries, the senior entrepreneurs are the fastest growing group and can make a significant contribution to the economy (Schott et al., 2017). It is likely that the attitude of senior entrepreneurs towards risk is going to be different to someone in their 20s and 30s. However, this may have a positive benefit in that the more considered approach to risk may lead to fewer failures. Khan (2013) found that businesses started by older entrepreneurs were more likely to survive for more than three years than their younger counterparts. There is also evidence to suggest that the senior entrepreneurs will invest more money in their business and this may also reduce the failure rate.

Conclusion

All entrepreneurs are different and there are many factors, both internal and external, that can influence them. Their personal background, family role models and education can all influence them.

References

Bosma, N. and Kelley, D. (2019). *Global Entrepreneurship Monitot 2018/2019 Global Report*. Babson Park: Global Entrepreneurship Research Association. www.gemconsortium.org

Chell, E. (1985). The entrepreneurial personality: A few ghosts laid to rest? *International Small Business Journal*, *3*(3), 43–54.

Khan, H. (2013). Five hours a day. Systemic innovation for an ageing population. London. Nesta. www.nesta.org

Say, J. B. (1836). *A treatise on political economy: Or the production, distribution, and consumption of wealth*. Grigg & Elliot.

Schøtt, T., Rogoff, E., Herrington, M., & Kew, P. (2017). GEM special report on senior entrepreneurship 2017. *Global Entrepreneurship Research Association, 56*. www.gemconsortium.org.

4 Opportunity recognition

Creativity and innovation

Summary

Opportunity recognition is an essential element in the entrepreneurial process. The three-step process starts with creativity; innovation is the refining and development of the idea and the final step is the commercialisation. The entrepreneur starts with an idea, which may be in response to the identification of a problem, e.g., a gap in the market. The next step is an evaluation of the opportunity, which can include an assessment of the market potential. This is usually in the form of gut instinct, a business plan or an opportunity business model. Intellectual property safeguards the idea through patent, trademarks, a registered design or copyright.

Introduction

This chapter looks at how entrepreneurs find ideas for their business and how to recognise opportunities. Entrepreneurs usually find a problem, for example, a product or service that doesn't exist or is not available in the way that they want. They then recognise that gap in the market as an opportunity that they can exploit. In order to develop the idea, they usually have to be creative and innovative for several reasons. The product or service has to be different enough to attract customers, the entrepreneur has to be able to develop the idea with few resources and, thirdly, it has to be viable from a business point of view.

The opportunity-recognition process usually follows the identification of a problem that can be identified as having the potential for a new venture. Ideas and solutions can be generated using creative thinking approaches such as mapping and brainstorming. Creativity can be developed as a process that can link the new concept to innovation.

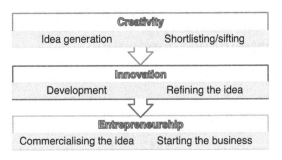

Figure 4.1 The three step process: creativity, innovation and entrepreneurship

The three-step process

The first step is creativity, where the entrepreneur will generate ideas. The majority of these ideas will not be taken any further. The next step is innovation, where the entrepreneur will develop the idea and make any alterations necessary to ensure that customers will buy the product or service. The final step is commercialising the idea and starting the business (Figure 4.1). However, even after the business has started, the entrepreneur will be continually developing. For example, Bloom and Wild had the concept of delivering the flowers through the letterbox, but didn't realise how important the technology was to their operations and had to make a substantial investment to ensure customers could order their flowers easily and smoothly.

According to DeTienne and Chandler (2004), creativity as a source of new ideas comes from grace, accident, personality, association and cognition. With regard to grace, ideas can come from nowhere, possibly by combining two components together. An example of this is the discovery of penicillin. There are many creative ideas, but very few are commercialised. For example, fewer than 5% of patents are commercialised.

Opportunity recognition

Opportunity recognition has been identified as one of the most important functions of successful entrepreneurs (Ardichvili et al., 2003). Entrepreneurs can spot an opportunity and turn it into a profitable business (Figure 4.2). Successful entrepreneurs can develop the idea and make changes until it works. Attitudes towards starting a business can depend on various factors, including an individual's own perception of the opportunities and their own skills and abilities. Other factors include the wider business environment in society such as attitudes towards failure and media attention towards entrepreneurship.

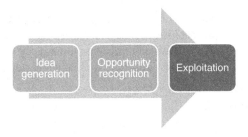

Figure 4.2 Opportunity recognition process

There are plenty of opportunities for starting a business. However, an entrepreneur will probably be able to start several businesses, possibly three or four during their working life. If one of these businesses is successful, then they will have rewards and recognition. Therefore, it is very important that entrepreneurs choose carefully before starting a business. Any business will have risks and these need to be managed in order to avoid failure.

Why do entrepreneurial opportunities exist?

Entrepreneurs are able to spot opportunities because they are alert to them and also because they have special knowledge. This knowledge can be gained as a result of work experience, education or travel or simply by looking for something that doesn't exist in the form that they are searching for. Knowledge is often in a very dispersed and incomplete form and entrepreneurs are able to make connections that do not occur to other people.

Sources of opportunity – where to start looking?

There are several ways to identify new opportunities. According to DeTienne and Chandler (2004), there are three main approaches that have been identified. These are active search, fortituous discovery and the creation of opportunities.

1   Active search

This view is consistent with the economic theory approach in that entrepreneurs take advantage of a shift in markets. Entrepreneurs are seen as having search skills that enable them to take steps to scan the environment and carry out a competitive analysis of the firms already in existence to identify the gap in the market.

2   Fortituous discovery

With this approach, the assumption is that entrepreneurs do not take an active search for opportunities but they are 'alert' to opportunities when they identify them. This allows entrepreneurs to be receptive to ideas and requires them to see the possibilities for a profitable business.

3   Opportunity creation

Some entrepreneurs can create something out of nothing. Handy's (2004) book, *The New Alchemists*, is a collection of case studies about people, not necessarily entrepreneurs, who have created something out of nothing. Schumpeter's view was that entrepreneurs can create new products and services as well as new markets and new forms of organisation.

Opportunity identification

How do entrepreneurs identify new opportunities? Some ideas are so good that they appear obvious. Although the source may be external, it's the entrepreneur's perception of the opportunities that's important. One of the areas that researchers have looked at is opportunity recognition. Baron and Ensley (2006) noted that some entrepreneurs can see connections between seemingly unrelated events or trends. In other words, they can 'connect the dots' between changes in demographics, markets, government policies, etc. The patterns they see will provide them with ideas for new products and services.

Opportunity recognition is often based on some existing knowledge or previous experience or a combination of the two. Baron and Ensley (2006) found that it is the inter-relationships between facts, figures and events that make the difference. They found that entrepreneurs adopt a pattern recognition perspective, which helps entrepreneurs recognise specific opportunities. Economists such as Kirzner found that 'alertness to opportunities' is what makes a person entrepreneurial.

Entrepreneurs may get their ideas from different sources including newspapers, magazines and business networks. Ideas may come from specialised sources, whereas some entrepreneurs have developed products through trial and error. Other entrepreneurs may have a very systematic approach and use techniques such as brainstorming, although there are many examples of where a random approach has been successful. One of the best places to start is with the entrepreneur's own skills and interests. These may be very specialised skills or they can be general skills such as marketing or financial skills.

Factors for opportunity recognition

1 Prior knowledge
2 Ability to recognise patterns in unrelated events
3 Unique life experiences
4 Technical abilities
5 Relevant training

Adapted from Baron and Ensley (2006)

Steps in the process

One of the important elements for an entrepreneur is the choice of the opportunity. Some entrepreneurs will have sifted through a range of possible options before deciding on the actual idea to pursue. Others may have already started a business and failed before starting a successful new venture. However, the sifting process is an important step that the entrepreneur goes through in evaluating the opportunities until the final idea is chosen (Figure 4.3).

Entrepreneurs can develop a solution to problems they have encountered; for example, Nick Woodman wanted to film his extreme sports and developed the GoPro camera. Nutella was created by Michele Ferrero's parents in response to rationing after the Second World War. These problems were identified by the entrepreneurs as opportunities to develop a product. Both the GoPro camera and Nutella were developed over time as the entrepreneurs tweaked them to make them more attractive to customers. Michele Ferrero added vegetable oil to his parents' recipe to make the chocolate spreadable.

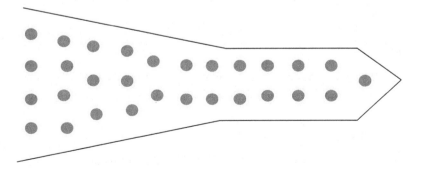

Figure 4.3 The innovation funnel

Case study: GoPro

The GoPro camera is popular with extreme sports enthusiasts who want to record their activities. This innovation made its founder, Nicholas Woodman, a billionaire. The camera can be used to record activities such as surfing, mountain biking and skiing. The camera can record videos or photographs at timed intervals. One of the reasons for the success of GoPro was its price. The GoPro Hera is priced around £100, although there are more expensive versions.

Nick Woodman had set up a business before. His previous venture was a website call Funberg, which was a gaming platform with cash prizes. He raised nearly $4 million but the company failed and it was one of the dot-com era's biggest failure stories. To recover, Nick Woodman went travelling to Indonesia and Australia. He wanted a camera that he could strap onto his wrist when he went surfing. He used rubber bands and other ties to strap a camera on to his wrist and he decided to build a camera that has a wrist strap and a casing all in one.

The first prototype was made using his mother's sewing machine and a drill. The cameras were initially sold in specialist surfing shops. They were also sold on the television shopping channel QVC.

Nick Woodman raised the initial start-up costs by selling 600 belts from Indonesia and he and his girlfriend made a profit of $10,000. His parents then invested a substantial amount of money (his father was an investment banker). He then raised venture capital from various sources and he saw his share of the company valued at $1 billion. By 2012, the company had sold over 2 million cameras and the business was floated in 2014.

For discussion

1   How did an earlier failure help Nick Woodman make a success of GoPro?
2   How did he keep the overheads down in the beginning and how important was this?

Exercise

•   What was innovative about GoPro and what were the key differentiating factors?

Innovation

Entrepreneurs are considered essential for innovation. Although much attention has been given to high-technology firms, entrepreneurs can be creative and innovative in all types of businesses. However, high-technology firms tend to grow faster and create more jobs than other types of businesses.

Opportunity evaluation

Choosing the right opportunity is very important for the entrepreneur, otherwise he/she will run out of cash due to insufficient sales. Some of the elements to examine to check if the opportunity is viable include the following: many large companies get so large that they find it difficult to keep close to the customer. This opens up opportunities for entrepreneurs to start a business to exploit these gaps.

Elements of the opportunity evaluation process:

- Product or service concept
- Management experience
- Competitive advantage
- Business model
- Timing and geographical focus
- Scale of funding

Market potential

One of the first steps is to ensure that there is a growing market. It is much easier to grow a business when the market is growing, rather than one where there is a contraction. One example of a declining market is high street shopping. Although there has been a change in shopping habits with the rapid increase of large out-of-town stores and online shopping, there may still be opportunities for a niche retailer. However, it is likely to prove a considerable challenge because of the declining footfall in the high street.

Other factors include market structure, market size and growth rate. Market share may also be important, especially if there is a well-known brand with a larger market share. Competitors may also be a factor to consider, especially if the market is over saturated.

Case study: Nutella

Pietro Ferrero and his wife Piera had a small café in Northern Italy and, in the 1940s, with food rationing, chocolate was in scarce supply. Pietro started adding hazelnuts to cocoa powder to make a chocolate spread. The chocolate spread was not new, as it had been available earlier in Italy. Pietro's version was not spreadable and it was only when his son, Michele Ferrero, added vegetable oil and put it in glass jars that it became popular (Figure 4.4). The brand itself was established in 1964 and Nutella is popular all over the world. The company also owns other well-known brands including Kinder Eggs, Tic Tac and Ferrero Rocher.

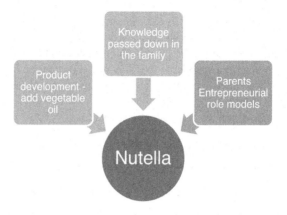

Figure 4.4 Opportunity development for Nutella

The recipe for Nutella is a secret and Michele Ferrero, who is credited with developing the company to the global brand it is today, was, at one time, the richest man in Italy. The company is one of the world's biggest consumer of hazelnuts, the key ingredient in its main products. The knowledge of how to make the initial chocolate spread was in the family. Ferrero's parents were running their own business and were entrepreneurial role models for him. He kept the recipe a secret and developed the brand.

For discussion

1   How did Michele Ferrero develop Nutella?
2   How important was his background and the knowledge developed by his parents?

Exercise

•   Identify other products where the recipe is secret and discuss why that is important for the brand.

Sources of business ideas

Ideas and solutions to problems can be generated using creative thinking approaches. For example, entrepreneurs can use techniques such as mapping to explore problems, opportunities and resources. Creativity can be seen as a structured process that connects ideas with innovation.

One of the main sources of business ideas is change. For example, changes occur in demography, customers' tastes and expectations, technology and politics. Any changes in the way people live and work will open up new markets or changes in fashions. Changes in markets can open up new opportunities such as online shopping. Changes in legislation can also provide opportunities, for example, changes in health and safety regulations. Other sources of ideas include products or services that are not available in one area but have been seen elsewhere, possibly in another country.

Vision and opportunity recognition

A key skill for entrepreneurs is to identify market drivers and recognise opportunities that these make possible. There are three approaches that can help the entrepreneur identify which business idea will convert into a real business opportunity:

Entrepreneurial vision – three approaches

1   Gut instinct. This can be based on experience and specialist knowledge about the market and the trends. However, although this approach is the one adopted by many entrepreneurs, it can be difficult to explain to banks and investors.
2   Traditional business plan. The business plan is useful to develop a new business idea, as it provides clear articulation of the concept. It is usually required by banks and other lenders and investors. However, business plans often do not convey the vision that the entrepreneur has for a business and it may also restrict the entrepreneurial spirit if investors want to stick to the original business plan.
3   Opportunity business model. The opportunity business model is a working version of a business plan. It shows how revenue and profits will be created. The key components and function are identified and related to financial performance. The opportunity business model is a clear and concise way to communicate an entrepreneurial opportunity. It can also help to improve the entrepreneur's own understanding of the underlying concept.

The business plan

The business plan can be used to develop a strategy for the business. Most banks and other finance providers will ask for a business plan that outlines a three- or five-year plan for the business. Entrepreneurs can also use the business plan to guide their strategy and measure performance (Figure 4.5).

Executive summary	• Short and factual, emphasize differentiation, key facts, • Stress quality of management
Company overview and background	• Details of the rationale for the idea/concept • Company history if it's already in existence
Products and Services	• Description of the products and/or services • Unique selling point of the products or services
Marketing and Sales	• Information about the size of the market and prospects for expansion • Identification of the customer and an analysis of the competition
Production and Operations	• Description of how the product is made/service is going to be delivered • Facilities, premises and equipment needed
Organisation and Management	• Organisational structure and responsibilities • Identify key personnel
Funding requirements	• Detail how much funding is required • Sources of funding already available
Financial Forecasts	• Summary of financial forecasts in the business plan • Sensitivity and ration analysis
Appendices	• Detailed financial projections • Other relevant information

Figure 4.5 Contents of the business plan

Key elements of the business plan:

• Does the plan show clearly the key elements of the business concept?
• Have the risks been identified and what steps have been taken to mini-mise them?
• Are the financial assumptions realistic?

Executive summary

The executive summary is one of the most important items in a business plan and it's very important to get this right. A summary should contain all the key elements in the business plan, including the description of the product or service, target market, price and promotion, financial highlights, including how much investment is required, and the potential profits.

Executive summary check list:

• Is it clear and exciting?
• Is it effective as a stand-alone document?
• Does it contain all the key elements of the business plan?
• Is it short and concise?

Company overview and background

This section provides the overview of the rationale for concept and the history of the idea, i.e., how was it developed and why. If the business is already established, then this section should contain a brief history, together with a summary of the financial performance. This section should also include the overall strategy and objectives.

Products and services

A full description of the product or service can be provided in this section, identifying the USP (unique selling point), i.e., what is unique about this product and what differentiates it from the competitors. Other elements to be included in this section include stage of development, pricing and legal issues, for example, any licences required.

Marketing and sales

This marketing section should include the marketing strategy, knowledge of the market, competitor analysis, sales/promotion and the target customers. What is the size of the market and is it growing? What are the barriers to entry? Who are the competitors and what is their strength and weakness?

Production and operations

The operations section needs to have the plan for production of a product or delivery of a service, including identification of the resources required. This section needs to include a full description, including the features and benefits, the stage of development as well as information on intellectual property rights.

Organisation and management

The management of the business is a very important element, as entrepreneurs who are good managers are more likely to succeed. This section will include details of key individuals, the organisational structure and also any nonexecutive directors.

Funding requirements

Details of the funding required, the type of financing, what it's going to be used for and exit routes for investors.

Financial forecasts

The detailed financial forecasts, i.e., the detailed monthly cash flow and profit and loss spreadsheets, can be put in the appendix. However, the summary of these forecasts need to be in the main body of the business plan.

The financial forecasts should be presented in a spreadsheet format with clear headings and totals. The profit and loss and cash flow forecasts need to be detailed and comprehensive in months, with annual totals. The balance sheet forecast only needs to be on an annual basis.

All the financial forecasts need to have any assumptions clearly outlined, e.g., any allowance for inflation, etc. The forecasts can also be tweaked for sensitivity analysis, for example, a forecast for a hotel could have two different forecasts: a pessimistic occupancy rate of 40% and an optimistic occupancy rate of 70%.

If the purpose of the business plan is to raise finance for the business, then the proposal to investors need to be outlined, indicating how much is needed, the return on investment (ROI) and possible exit strategies.

Check list for the business plan

1   Is the business viable? Is the business concept sustainable and does it have a competitive advantage?
2   Would an investor be interested in funding this business? What are the key financial elements?
3   What is the target market? Is the market need clearly presented and the typical customer identified?
4   What is the unique selling point (USP)? What is different about this product or service that will appeal to customers?
5   Does the management team have the skills to run this business efficiently and effectively? What is their track record? Have they got relevant skills and experience?
6   Are the financial forecasts correct and accurate? Does the business plan show a clear understanding of the financial requirements of the business?
7   Is this business scalable? Can the concept be replicated elsewhere? Does the business plan show a clear understanding of developing a brand?

Problem areas to avoid:

1   Lack of clear strategy and vision
2   Too much detail – keep it clear and simple
3   Very little management expertise and relevant experience and knowledge
4   Unrealistic monthly financial forecasts

Successful business plans have a combination of the following:

•   Enthusiastic and committed entrepreneurs
•   Excellent management team

- Sustainable business model
- Competitive advantage
- Opportunities to expand the business
- Exit strategies, e.g., flotation
- Risks understood and mitigated

One of the fundamental elements in the business plan, both for the entrepreneur and the investor, is to ensure that there is sufficient cash flow in the business to ensure its survival. Presenting a good business plan is essential to raising financing and it's also important for the entrepreneur to show an understanding of financial management and that all the risks have been covered.

Case study: Bloom and Wild

Flowers have traditionally been delivered in a large box or a container and this is expensive. Bloom and Wild deliver flowers in a box that fits through a normal letter box. This is a simple solution and reduces the cost of delivery. In addition, no one has to be at home to take delivery of the flowers. The company was founded by Aron Gelbard and Ben Stanway in 2013. After graduating from Jesus College, Oxford, Gelbard went to work as a management consultant. He knew he wanted to be an entrepreneur and his inspiration was one of his friends at university, Anthony Fletcher, who founded Graze, which was a pioneer of letterbox delivery. Bloom and Wild became one of the fastest growing companies in the UK and the company is constantly innovating to see what can be fit through a letterbox, including some items that didn't suit this type of delivery, including orchids and Christmas wreaths.

For discussion

1   Why is letterbox delivery increasing in popularity?
2   What is to stop competitors copying this idea?

Exercise

- What other products would be suitable for this form of delivery?

The opportunity business model

The business opportunity model is considered to be a more dynamic approach to the formal business plan. The focus is on how the revenues and the profits will be generated, the value added, innovation and the customers.

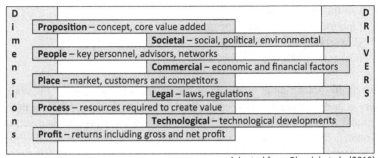

Adapted from Blundel et al., (2018)

Figure 4.6 The opportunity business model

This approach was developed in the 1990s in the dot-com boom and the more recent developments included the identification of the key dimensions and the drivers (Blundel et al., 2017). The dimensions include the proposition, the people, the place, the process and the profit (Figure 4.6).

The value proposition is what the concept offers that is not available elsewhere. This dimension identifies the problem or the need that it solves for the customer. The people are the key personnel who may have special knowledge or expertise that is essential. The place is the target market, customers and competitors. The process is the equipment, infrastructure and technology and needs to be in place. The profit includes the cost structure, the margins including items such as stock turnover.

The drivers are the external factors that affect the business including societal, commercial, legal and technological issues. The drivers are the changes in the economy, in demography, in the business environment, in the political and legal matters and in technology. For example, the availability of Apple apps enabled Uber to be developed.

Case study: the Instant Pot Cooker

The Instant Pot Cooker, which was launched in 2010, became the top selling product in the US on Amazon. It outsold electronic products such as tablets and TVs. It became a success through social media word-of-mouth and recipes were shared online by fans who shared their cooking tips.

Robert Wang wanted to make it easier to cook a meal. He brainstormed the idea with a friend in Canada, where they both lived. He realised that people were looking for the same thing as they were, a way to cook meals for the family that were quick and affordable. The Instant Pot Cooker is based on the pressure cooker but can be used as a slow cooker. It can speed up the cooking process and it is also preprogrammed for cooking items such as soup and porridge. It is also priced affordably and the marketing strategy was to expand by word-of-mouth rather than spend on advertising.

For discussion

1 How did Robert Wang come up with the idea of a pressure cooker?
2 Was social media the best way to promote this product?
3 Why was word-of-mouth appropriate for this Instant Pot Cooker?

Exercise

• Robert Wang based his idea on a pressure cooker. What are the differences between a pressure cooker and an Instant Pot Cooker that made it a success?

Assessing opportunities

Many brilliant business ideas often fail or struggle to survive in the very competitive and rapidly changing markets. Exploiting an opportunity is part of the entrepreneurial process and entrepreneurs have to combine creativity and innovation with determination. This can be a time consuming and expensive process that can result in some unpredictable and surprising developments. There are many examples of entrepreneurs who have developed a product or a service and nearly failed only to see it succeed in another market or at a different time.

Intellectual property

Innovations and ideas need to be safeguarded in order to prevent copycats. A patent is designed to protect a new invention. If a patent is granted, it lasts for 20 years and enables the entrepreneur to take legal action if someone tries to copy it. A trademark is a sign, a logo or both, which distinguishes the business from its competitors. Once registered, these must be renewed every 10 years. A registered design can give protection to the appearance of a product. Copyright allows the entrepreneur to protect original work, e.g., songs and books. Creators must record and retain proof of ownership.

• **Patents** – gives exclusive rights for 20 years, but is complex and costly
• **Trademarks** – can protect your name and brand
• **Registered design** – provides design right of ownership for up to 25 years
• **Copyright** – similar to above, 25 to 70 years protection depending on type of work

References

Ardichvili, A., Cardozo, R., & Ray, S. (2003). A theory of entrepreneurial opportunity identification and development. *Journal of Business Venturing, 18*(1), 105–123.

Baron, R. A., & Ensley, M. D. (2006). Opportunity recognition as the detection of meaningful patterns: Evidence from comparisons of novice and experienced entrepreneurs. *Management Science, 52*(9), 1331–1344.

Blundel, R., Lockett, N., & Wang, C. (2018). *Exploring entrepreneurship*. Sage Publications.

DeTienne, D. R., & Chandler, G. N. (2004). Opportunity identification and its role in the entrepreneurial classroom: A pedagogical approach and empirical test. *Academy of Management Learning & Education, 3*(3), 242–257.

Handy, C. B. (2004). *The new alchemists*. London. Hutchinson.

5 Enterprise culture

Summary

Entrepreneurs can reinvigorate the economy and introduce new ideas and developments and, consequently, governments have strategies to create an enterprise culture all over the world. In order to facilitate an enterprise culture, governments will aim to provide suitable infrastructure, support policies and address market failure for finance, especially venture capital. An entrepreneurial ecosystem is wider in concept and includes the social and political environment as well as the cultural norms. Government support is targeted at small businesses and the Bolton report in 1971 raised awareness and introduced definitions for different sectors. The EU definition of small business is fewer than 50 employees, and a micro business has less than 10. Small and medium-sized enterprises account for 99% of private sector businesses in the UK and almost half of the number of jobs. The majority of small businesses in the UK do not employ anyone else. Some regions are more entrepreneurial than others, with London, the South-East and the South-West having the highest rates of business density. Some of the approaches taken by the UK government to encourage an enterprise culture include reducing the bureaucracy, skills training, access to finance, reducing the fear of failure and support for innovation.

Introduction

Successive governments in the UK and in other countries have stated that their aim is to create an entrepreneurial culture. The motivation for making a country or a region more entrepreneurial is to create employment, regenerate a region or to diversify the economy. Entrepreneurs can also reinvigorate an economy and bring in new ideas and developments.

Entrepreneurship is one of the fundamental elements in all economies. The majority of large multinational companies have started out as small enterprises, the vision of one or two entrepreneurs. Successful entrepreneurs can reap financial rewards as well as be recognised for their achievements and contribution to society. However, there are also very many entrepreneurs who operate on a very small scale, often barely making a living.

There are many factors that can affect the entrepreneurial culture. These include the availability of finance, government support and policies, education, research and development, the physical infrastructure and cultural norms. Cultural norms can affect the perception of entrepreneurship and whether entrepreneurs are respected in their society. This is difficult to change in the short term, as attitudes can be developed over decades, or possibly centuries, in a country or a region.

Entrepreneurial ecosystem

In recent years, there has been an increasing awareness of the impact of the environmental influences on entrepreneurial success. An entrepreneurial ecosystem is the external environment than supports and encourages entrepreneurship in a geographical area. It also includes the institutional and cultural processes that support and encourage new business creation and growth. The ecosystem is considered more comprehensive than a cluster in a geographical area because it is based on the context in which the business operates.

Creating an enterprise culture

Entrepreneurship and small businesses have become an important aspect of government policies, as there has been an increasing awareness of their contribution to the economy. Entrepreneurial new ventures create a large proportion of the new jobs in an economy and small businesses employ approximately half the workforce. Not only do entrepreneurs create jobs, they also create social mobility.

Governments aim to create an enterprise culture in order to encourage business start-ups and growth. One of the ways that governments will help is by reducing bureaucracy. There is recognition that some employment legislation will have an adverse effect on smaller firms. The UK government has stated that it intends to reduce bureaucracy for small firms and provide other support, such as finance and grants.

The UK government provides different kinds of support for small businesses, including advice, finance, training, export advice and other support. Large firms dominated the economy until the 1960s, when there was an increasing recognition of the importance of small firms. From the late 1960s, there was a shift in the focus towards small businesses and the role of the government in creating an enterprise culture. One of the main justifications for government intervention is market failure, e.g., in venture capital where businesses are too small to justify the investment.

Case study: David Davies (Davies the Ocean)

David Davies from Llandinam, near Newtown in mid Wales, is an example of how an entrepreneur can transform the regional economy. He was the son of a sawyer and he began work as a workman and then became a railway contractor. He built the railway from Newtown to Machynlleth and had to dig out a very difficult cutting. He also built the railway from Lampeter to Aberystwyth across Tregaron Bog, another challenge, which necessitated buying wool from the local sheep to lay the track.

The cutting in Talerddig almost bankrupted him because the rock was so hard and it was so difficult. However, he managed to sell the stone from the cutting for making roads and became the first millionaire in Wales. He went on to buy a coal mine and he built the docks in Barry in South Wales to export the coal. The coal mine was called the Ocean Mine and he became known as Davies the Ocean. The docks in Barry were also a major contributor to the export of coal. He donated £5,000 in the 1870s to establish the University of Wales in Aberystwyth.

For discussion

1   How did David Davies transform the local economy in Mid and South Wales?
2   The rock would have been a major set-back for most people. What do his actions say about David Davies?

Exercise

•   Identify other examples where waste products can be used for other purposes.

Small and medium-sized enterprises

Small and medium-sized enterprises create almost half the jobs in the private sector. They also create the majority of new jobs. Anyone can start a business, regardless of their age, education, sex and employment background, etc. Although most of the small businesses in the UK do not employ another person, they generate still generate substantial tax receipts for the government.

One of the most important contributions of the Bolton report in 1971 was raising the awareness of the comparison of small businesses in the UK to other countries. There were concerns that the levels of creation of new businesses were declining and that there was a need to create an enterprise culture. The Bolton report identified the importance of new enterprises for the health of the economy as they were the 'seedbed' of economic development. The report stated, 'We believe that the health of the economy requires the birth of new enterprises in substantial numbers (Bolton, 1971:85).' The report argued that new businesses are essential to a healthy economy, as they are the seedbed of larger firms and an economy dominated by large firms would stagnate.

The rise of large-scale manufacturing and improved production facilities had led to a decrease in employment in small firms by the late 1960s. The decline in the number of small firms had actually ended in the 1960s, and by the late 1980s the number employed in small firms had increased to the level they had been in the 1930s. There were regional differences in the rate of growth in the number of SMEs with London and the South-East having the highest rate of growth, followed by East Anglia and the South-West and then the Midlands. The lowest rate of SME growth was in the North-West of England Wales, Scotland and Northern Ireland.

The question of how many small firms there are in the UK is a difficult one, especially given the issues regarding the definition of a small business. Another problem is the data. There are several sources of data about small businesses but getting a complete dataset is almost impossible. The main source of data on small firms is VAT registration, the Companies House database and employment statistics. The VAT register is one of the most comprehensive databases and it provides data on turnover but not the number of employees. The other problem is that it does not provide data on firms that are below the threshold for VAT registration.

Since the 19th century, economists had focused on large firms and the theory of the firm in economics had been geared towards large businesses. By the late 1960s and early 1970s, there was concern that the numbers of small businesses were declining and that the situation was worse in the UK than in other countries. In fact, the decline in the number of small businesses had come to an end before the Bolton committee published its report and there was an increasing awareness of the importance of new ventures in creating employment.

There is no single definition of a small firm, mainly because of the wide diversity of businesses. The Bolton report defined a small firm as an independent business, managed by its owner or part-owners and having a small market share. The report used a number of different statistical definitions for different industries and recognised that size was relevant to sector. A mixture of employees and turnover was used.

However, no single definition can encompass what is considered to be a small business, mainly because of their diversity. These businesses can cover a wide range of enterprises including the small, independent hardware shop, the local car repair garage and the sewing machine repair workshop. The EU uses the term 'micro-businesses' to describe businesses with fewer than 10 employees.

Another problem for the government is counting the number of enterprises. Many small businesses do not register for VAT, which is one of the main sources of information. Some businesses have such a short lifespan that they cease trading before they register. The other problem is that small businesses are changing all the time, and this makes it difficult to estimate the size of the sector and the levels of employment generated.

The Bolton definitions were criticised, mainly on the basis of its definition of the management of the small firm, and research has shown that many small firms bring in professional managers at between 10 and 20 employees and, by the time a business gets to around 100 employees, managerial appointments would have been put in place, together with a formal management structure. The Bolton report's definitions were also criticised on the basis that small firms also have 'niche' markets and can provide a very specialised service or product, and, in fact, it is these companies that are most successful.

The message from the Bolton report was that something needed to be done to encourage entrepreneurship. By the 1980s, Margaret Thatcher was in power and the government introduced the enterprise initiatives that were designed to make people more 'enterprising.'

The statistical definition of a small business is one with fewer than 50 employees (Table 5.1). The term *small and medium-sized enterprises* (SMEs) is often used to those with fewer than 250 employees. The European Commission also has a definition of small businesses based on the number of employees, turnover, etc. The reason for the emphasis on the definitions of SMEs is that these businesses then qualify for entrepreneurial support. Firms that qualify are eligible for government support, tax and other benefits, and administrative exemptions. Other conditions also have to be fulfilled, e.g., the enterprise must be autonomous (not part of a larger group).

Table 5.1 EU definition of small businesses

Category	Employees	Turnover OR	Balance sheet
Medium	< 250	≤ €50 m	≤ €43 m
Small	< 50	≤ €10 m	≤ €10 m
Micro	< 10	≤ €2 m	≤ €2 m

Each day, some businesses start up and others are closed and this is known as the 'churn rate.' The reasons for closing a business can vary from retirement to finding a job, or other reasons. If the entrepreneur fails to make sufficient sales and profits, then the business will eventually collapse when there are insufficient funds to pay the bills. This can be a painful experience for the entrepreneurs, who may lose all their assets including their home.

One of problems with small business statistics is getting hold of up-to-date and accurate information about them and their employees. VAT registrations give an indication of the number but only for businesses with a turnover of over £85,000. Businesses have to register for VAT once the turnover is over the £85,000 threshold, but below that level VAT registration is voluntary.

Small businesses in the UK

In 2018, there were 5.7 million private sector businesses in the UK (Figure 5.1), a decrease of 27,000 compared to 2017. This is the first fall in the number of businesses since in 2000. However, in 2018 there were still 2.2 million more businesses than in 2000, an increase of 63% over the whole period. The number of nonemploying businesses decreased by 1%, but the number of employing businesses rose by 2%. However, 75% of all the businesses did not have any employees. SMEs provided 60% of the total private sector employment and the combined annual turnover was 52% of private sector turnover (BEIS, 2019).

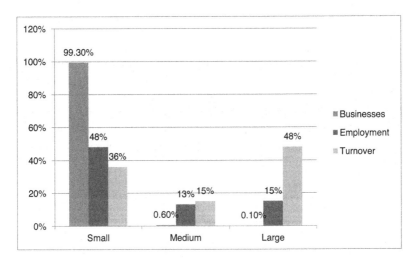

Figure 5.1 SMEs numbers, employment and turnover

There were 16.3 million people employed in SMEs in 2018, an increase of 1% since 2017 and the share of total employment in private sector businesses was 60%. Therefore, although the overall number of private-sector businesses decreased slightly, the overall employment in SMEs increased.

In the UK, there are three main legal forms of starting a new business:

- *Sole trader*

  A sole trader runs their own business as an individual and they are self-employed. The sole trader can keep all the profits of the business and is responsible for all the losses. There are statutory requirements to keep records of the business and to submit a self-assessment return every year. The sole trader can offset any costs incurred in running the business against tax.

- *Partnership*

  In a partnership, all the partners share the responsibilities of the business. This includes all losses and paying for any assets purchased by the business. The partners share the profits and pay tax on their share. One nominated partner is responsible for keeping the financial records and preparing the tax returns.

- *Directors in a limited company*

  A limited company can be set up to run a new business. This is a legal entity and is separate from the directors of the company. The company has shares and the directors have a legal responsibility to keep company records and file the accounts and the company tax return.

The majority of businesses (59%) in the UK in 2018 were sole proprietorships, 34% were companies and 7% were partnerships (Figure 5.2). Almost

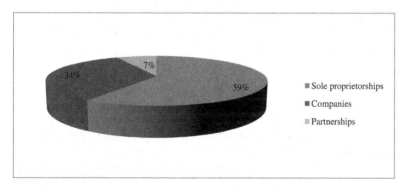

Figure 5.2 Legal forms of business

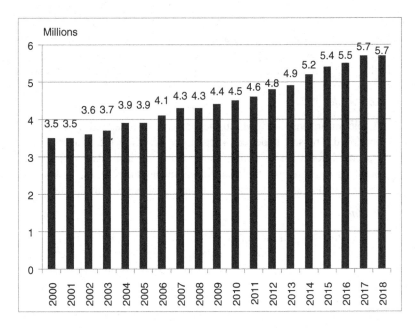

Figure 5.3 Trends in the business population since 2000

half of the companies did not have any employees and 248,000 sole proprietorships did have employees.

Since 2000, there had been a steady growth in the number of businesses in the UK (Figure 5.3). However, there was a fall of 27,000 between 2017 and 2018. The majority of the growth since 2000 has been due to an increase in businesses with no employees.

Twenty percent of SMEs were in the construction industry in 2018, 10% in wholesale and retail trade and 10% in the trade and repair sectors. With regard to employment, 14% of all SME employment was in the wholesale and trade sector.

Entrepreneurs in the UK by region

Some regions in the UK could be considered more entrepreneurial than others (Figure 5.4). London and the South East of England have a higher proportion of private businesses than the rest of the UK, with 35% in these areas. The North East had the lowest number of private sector businesses. London and the South East of England also had the highest rates of business density, i.e., the number of businesses per 10,000 resident adults (BEIS, 2019).

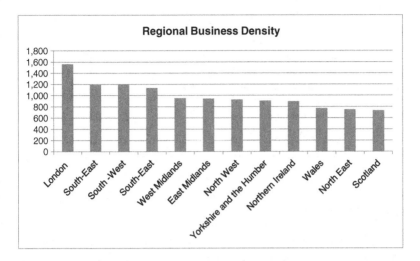

Figure 5.4 Business density per 10,000 adults
Source: BEIS (2019:10)

Government policy

In recent years, there has been a shift from start-ups and potential growth firms have been targeted for support. This is because growth firms have the most potential for creating employment. There has been more emphasis on training and advice as a result. The advice in recent years has been tailored towards the needs of the business and this has resulted in the growth of mentoring and consultancies.

The government report on 'Enterprise: Unlocking the UK's Talent' was published in March 2008. This outlined the UK government's vision to 'make the UK the most enterprising economy in the world and the best place to start a business.' The strategy outlined in the document states that the UK government wanted people to have more ambition to start a business.

In December 2013 the UK government launched its strategy 'Small Business: GREAT Ambition.' The aim of this was to take a 'long term approach to promote growth, job creation, boosting skills and making the UK more competitive (BIS, 2013:4).' This strategy was designed to help small businesses to grow.

Self-employment

Although self-employment is often used as a proxy for the entrepreneur in reality, some people may become self-employed because they cannot find a suitable job. In addition, some employers may only employ people

Table 5.2 Reasons for self-employment

Independence	30%
Nature of the occupation	21.5%
Other reasons	14.6%
More money	12.7%
Opportunity, availability of resources	12.5%
Redundancy	9,3%
Market demand	8.8%
Family business	6.9%

Source: Adapted from Dawson et al. (2009)

on a casual, self-employed basis and there are others who choose self-employment for taxation reasons.

The motivations to become self-employed can be divided into two types: those that have chosen self-employment voluntarily so that they can pursue entrepreneurial opportunities and those who do so out of necessity. There are also external influences on self-employment, such as the state of the economy and also rising house prices, which allow entrepreneurs invest spare equity into a business. Dawson et al. (2009) found that independence and work satisfaction was the main motivation followed by the nature of the occupation (Table 5.2). This could be because some occupations, such as accountants, solicitors and builders, are often self-employed. More women chose self-employment because of family commitments than men.

The large increase in the number of SMEs in the 1970s and 1980s was largely as a result in the increase of the self-employed. The number of self-employed increased from 1.92 million in 1979 to 3.3 million in 1990, an increase of nearly 80%. The majority of the self-employed do not have employees and the large increase in the number of self-employed contributed almost half of the increase in the number employed in SMEs with fewer than 20 employees.

Some groups are more likely to be self-employed, for example, construction workers and farmers. There are some minority groups that are also more likely to be self-employed such as those of Indian-Pakistani-Bangladeshi origin. Women are less likely to be self-employed, although there has been a considerable increase in recent years.

Market failure

The UK government spends billions of pounds every year developing an entrepreneurial culture. This support is usually justified because of three main arguments. The first one is that government initiatives are required because there are market failures that inhibit entrepreneurship. For example, the market for finance may leave some entrepreneurs without being able to raise the money that they need. The other argument is that they create new jobs. Other market failures include training, i.e., the government has to provide training because small firms do not have the necessary resources or skills. The other example of market failure is research and development, where entrepreneurs may be unable to make the necessary investments and need support to develop their products.

At the start of the 1980s, there were strong trade unions and some of the working practices that had been defended by them were considered inefficient. New businesses were seen as a source of new jobs and the 1980s were seen as the decade of enterprise. The basis for the development of the enterprise culture in the 1980s was that the unemployed should create their own jobs. This reflected a change in approach, in that small businesses were encouraged.

The 1980s also saw a decrease in employment in large firms. In the early 1980s, employment in large firms fell by around 50%, approximately 3.5 million employees. Changes in technology led to jobs being lost in manufacturing and the banking sector as companies made staff redundant to reduce costs. Large firms also started outsourcing their activities. The government's response was to encourage more people to become self-employed and start their own business. Changes in government policies were designed to help small businesses and changes in taxation and deregulation were also introduced.

The enterprise culture that was developed in the 1980s was based on the notion that the unemployed should be encouraged to create their own jobs. There was a change in attitude towards supporting and encouraging entrepreneurs to create new businesses. The Enterprise Initiatives in the 1980s included the Enterprise Allowance Scheme. This was an innovative scheme that was targeted specifically at the unemployed to become self-employed. If someone is unemployed for six months, then they qualify for the enterprise allowance scheme.

Other initiatives in the 1980s to create an enterprise culture included the Enterprise Initiative to provide management consultancy for small firms. Other important developments included the Loan Guarantee Scheme and the Business Expansion Scheme.

By the 1990s, the policy had changed from encouraging start-ups to targeting businesses with growth potential. This is because they were seen as more likely to create employment. Other developments included advice tailored for businesses, rather than a one-size-fits-all approach, as well as more mentoring and consultancies.

The current policy is to provide signposting, through the gov.uk webpage, to the sources of advice and support available. Gov.uk is an information website that provides information about government support. Topics include starting up, finance and grants, tax and payroll and marketing, etc.

Problems

One of the complaints about government support for small business is that there are too many initiatives and this has led to confusion on the part of the small business owner-manager. The result is that few businesses approach government agencies for assistance. Another complaint is that there is some variation in the quality of the support that is available. When entrepreneurs approach government support agencies for advice, they also complain about the unnecessary bureaucracy.

Doug Richard, who was formerly one of the dragons on the BBC2 television series *Dragons' Den*, was commissioned to look at government support for small businesses. Richard, 2008:4 found a system that was "overly complex, ineffective and undirected". Over 3,000 support schemes were run by 2,000 public bodies at a cost of at least £2 bn. The total direct public expenditure on small business was estimated at £10–£12 billion and he estimated that at least one-third of the money was wasted.

'Enterprise: Unlocking the UK's Talent' March 2008

By 2008, there were concerns that entrepreneurship in other countries was much higher than in the UK. In its report on 'Enterprise, Unlocking the UK's Talent,' the government strategy for enterprise noted that the US had 20% more businesses per head than in the UK. In addition, new businesses in the UK were also likely to grow more slowly than in the US, where more businesses were achieving high growth. Established businesses were also less likely to expand, with one-third saying they had no ambition to grow. It was also found that fear of failure was higher in the UK than in the US, with 36% people saying it would prevent them from starting a business compared to 21% in the US.

The vision in this report was 'to make the UK the most enterprising economy in the world and the best place to start a business (BERR, 2008:5).' The aims of the strategy were to want 'more people to have the ambition to start and grow businesses, having access to suitable business advice and finance and enabled by a strong regulatory framework' (BERR, 2008:5).

One of the key issues that was identified in the strategy was the fear of failure (Table 5.3). The regulations were then changed so that insolvency officers were given discretion over whether or not to place an advert in the local press. The aim of this was to reduce the embarrassment and risk of stigma in the

Table 5.3 The five enablers

1	**Culture**	Developing entrepreneurship and reducing the fear of failure
2	**Knowledge and skillss**	More external advice and more training for workforce and managers
3	**Access to finance**	Access to appropriate finance and make the businesses 'investment ready'
4	**Regulatory framework**	Targeted net reduction in the administrative burden by 25%
5	**Business innovation**	New innovation strategy, more investment in R & D, more innovation partnerships between businesses and businesses and universities

local community and the fear of failure. Another aim was to inspire young people about enterprise and plans were announced to promote enterprise through football clubs.

'Small Business: GREAT Ambition'

In 2014, the UK government launched its 'Small Business: GREAT Ambition' strategy, stating that its aim was to make it easier for small businesses to grow and to scale up. In order to achieve this, the intention was to make it easier to achieve the following:

- Finance for growth
- Develop new ideas
- Hire people
- Expand into new markets

There was also a commitment to make it easier to get support and to cut red tape.

Financial support

There was a growing concern about the shortage of equity finance available for small businesses. The UK government identified an 'equity gap' between £50,000 and £500,000 as the difference between the equity that friends and family can provide and the funding that can be raised from private equity or floating the company on the stock exchange.

The British Business Bank was established in 2012 to bring together several of the UK government's financial support schemes for small businesses (Table 5.4). The aim of the British Business Bank is to increase the supply of

Table 5.4 Government sources of finance

Scheme	Maximum amounts	Conditions
Enterprise Investment Scheme	£12 million	Trading for seven years, fewer than 250 employees and less than £15 million gross assets
Seed Enterprise Investment Scheme	£150,000	Not previously carried out a different trade, fewer than 25 employees and less than £200,000 gross assets
Social Investment Tax Relief		Registered charity, community interest company or community benefit company, fewer than 250 employees and less than £15 million gross assets
Venture Capital Trust	£12 million	Trading for less than seven years, fewer than 250 employees and less than £15 million gross assets

finance where markets aren't working and to provide more options and a more diverse financial market.

The Enterprise Finance Guarantee Scheme is available to businesses which are unable to raise money due to an insufficient track record or lack of security. The founders of Innocent, for example, were unable to raise the finance to start their business and they used the Enterprise Finance Guarantee Scheme. The scheme is run in conjunction with high street banks. The business must be viable, i.e., able to meet interest and capital repayments. The amounts available are between £1,000 and £1.2 million and the repayment period can be up to 10 years.

The UK government currently has four schemes to help SMEs raise venture capital. They offer tax relief to investors. The business must be UK based, have a qualifying trade, e.g., hotels are excluded and not be controlled by another company.

Budgets

Announcements to help and support small businesses are often included in the UK government's budgets. In the 2011 budget, the UK government announced its intention to make the UK 'the best place in Europe to start, finance and grow a business (Budget, 2011:1).' For example, in order to reduce bureaucracy, micro-businesses and new start-ups were exempted from domestic regulation from 1 April 2011 for 3 years. The Enterprise Investment Scheme (EIS) and Venture Capital Trust were updated and the SME rate of R & D tax credit was increased to 200% from April 2011 and 225% from April 2012. The small business rate relief holiday extended for one year from 1 October 2011.

The 2012 budget announced that, from April 2013, small firms with a turnover of up to £77,000 per year would be allowed to change their accounting from accrual to cash basis. Small firms then only have to pay tax on the amount of money they have received. Accrual accounting usually means an accountant has to be involved, whereas cash accounting means a small firm can prepare the accounts themselves. The integration of tax and NI was also announced. Loans for young entrepreneurs aged between 18 and 25 to borrow £5,000–£10,000 for a new business idea were also announced.

In 2016, the chancellor announced a new £15,000 threshold for small business rate relief, more than double the previous level of £6,000. He also increased the higher rate from £18,000 to £51,000, and said the changes mean 600,000 small firms will pay no business rates at all. New £1,000 online allowances for people who rent out their homes and make money through sharing economy platforms were introduced.

References

BEIS, (2019). 'Business Population Estimates for the UK and the Regions', 2018. Department for Business, Energy & Industrial Strategy, London. Retrieved from www.gov.uk

Bennett, R. (2008). SME policy support in Britain since the 1990s: What have we learnt? *Environment and Planning C: Government and Policy, 26*(2), 375–397.

BERR, (2008). 'Enterprise: Unlocking the UK's Talent'. Department for Business, Enterprise and Regulatory Reform. H.M. Treasury. Retrieved from www.gov.uk

BIS, (2013). 'Small business: GREAT ambition'. Department for Business, Innovation and Skills. Retrieved from www.gov.uk

Dawson, C. J., Henley, A., & Latreille, P. L. (2009). *Why do individuals choose self-employment?* Retrieved from www.econstor.eu/bitstream/10419/35711/1/592883760.pdf

Federation of Small Businesses (2013). *Enterprise 2050: Getting UK enterprise policy right*. London: Federation of Small Businesses.

Gavron, R. (1998). *The entrepreneurial society*. London: Institute for Public Policy Research.

Richard, D., (2008), Small Business and Government: The Richard Report. Submission to Shadow Cabinet. London.

Storey, D. J. (1994, 2016). *Understanding the small business sector*. Abingdon, UK: Routledge.

6   Female entrepreneurship

Summary

There has been an increasing interest in recent years in the contribution that female and minority entrepreneurs can make to the economy. There are concerns that they face additional hurdles in starting a business, especially raising finance. They may also have less confidence and are less likely to build networks, which can result in a lower growth potential. Female entrepreneurs are gradually catching up with men, although there has been a reduction between 2016 and 2018 in the UK. Women are more likely to focus on the health and education sectors. They are also more likely to cite family reasons for becoming self-employed. There have been some criticisms of the underperformance approach of women-led businesses compared to their male counterparts and that this gendered approach may not be relevant. Women generally rely on more accessible forms of finance, such as credit cards. They may have lower levels of savings to invest in a new business due to the gender pay gap. Venture capitalists tend to focus on technology and women are less likely to start a business in this sector. Although equal numbers of women study science and technology subjects up to degree level, the number of women registering patents is very low compared to men. Some ethnic minority groups, such as those of Pakistani origin, are more entrepreneurial than others. They are also more likely to be financed by family and friends. The businesses founded by ethnic minorities often tend to focus on particular sectors, such as restaurants and trade with their own ethnic group. Other under-represented groups include the disabled and ex-offenders.

Introduction

In recent years, there has been a growing interest in encouraging diversity in entrepreneurship. This is because female and minority entrepreneurs, as well as other under-represented groups, have the potential to create jobs and increase the GDP of a region or country. However, these groups may face additional hurdles to starting a business, especially raising finance. Despite enormous changes in equality and an increased participation in the workplace, women are still less likely to start a business. If they do start a business, they tend to be smaller and employ fewer people than those run by men. Another issue that may affect the likelihood of women starting a business is the lack of confidence in their management skills. Women are also less likely to network with other entrepreneurial role models. Women-led businesses are more likely to be in certain sectors, such as health and beauty. These service sectors have low barriers to entry, which can result in high levels of competition, which can lead to lower growth prospects.

Female entrepreneurs

According to the Global Entrepreneurship Monitor (GEM), women are catching up with men, although there is a greater involvement in entrepreneurship by men than women in most countries. The rate of female entrepreneurship varies considerably in different countries. Kelley et al. (2011) found that, although women's motivations for starting a business were the same as for men, their attitudes towards entrepreneurship and the industries they operated in and their ambitions for growth were very different. Women in sub-Saharan Africa, for example, are more likely to be motivated by necessity, whereas women in Asia are more likely to be motivated by opportunity. The Global Entrepreneurship Monitor asks entrepreneurs how many employees they currently have and how many they expect to have in the next five years. The difference between current and expected, according to GEM, gives growth expectations. The results show that women in sub-Saharan Africa have low growth expectations, with only 5% expecting to employ more than 20 in the next five years. This is despite the high participation of women in early-stage entrepreneurial activity.

Men are now twice as likely to be more entrepreneurial than women, but in 2001 they were two-and-a-half times more likely to be entrepreneurial, i.e., involved in the early stages of a new venture. Women account for less than a third of those in self-employment, but over half the increase in self-employment since the 2008 recession. Lower female self-employment rates may reflect sectoral distribution, problems in raising finance and that they may have other responsibilities, e.g., childcare. Women account for 17% of business owners/managers/employers.

The GEM report (2019) found that only nine economies out of 47 showed equal or higher early-stage entrepreneurship between men and women. These were Indonesia, Thailand, Panama, Qatar, Madagascar, Kazakstan, Ecuador, Vietnam and Angola. In other countries such as Sweden, Turkey,

Greece and Switzerland, women started businesses at half the rate of men. Figure 6.2 shows the higher participation of women in entrepreneurship in sub-Saharan Africa and Latin America.

Women-led businesses

In the UK, it was estimated that women-led SMEs contributed approximately £85 billion to the economy in 2017. Nineteen percent of SME employers were led by women, a reduction of 2% in two years since 2015. The Rose Review (2019) pointed out that only 6% of women in the UK run their own business compared to 15% in Canada and, for every 10 male entrepreneurs, there are between four and five female entrepreneurs. Although women are as successful as men in sustaining the business over time, only 13% achieve a turnover of over £1 million compared to 29% of male entrepreneurs.

One of the issues for female entrepreneurs is that there is an apparent bias within the venture capital system. Only 1% of UK venture capital is invested in women-led businesses which accounts for 4% of the deals. This is because approximately half the investment teams have no women at all and only 13% of the senior investors are women. According to the Rose Review (2019), if women started businesses at the same rate as men and had the same rate of growth, around £250 billion could be added to the Gross Value Added of the economy.

Figure 6.1 shows that the percentage of women starting a business in the UK increased steadily from 2007 to 2012. However, there has been a slight decline between 2016 and 2017, increasing the gap between male and female entrepreneurs.

Female entrepreneurs' businesses tend to be in different sectors to those run by men. Women are more likely to be in health services and education, comprising 52% and 50% respectively. They are less likely to run businesses in the manufacturing and the information and communication sectors, with only 12% and 11% of businesses led by women, respectively.

Other factors that may affect the decision to start a business include lower self-confidence or greater risk aversion, which may particularly affect women (Table 6.1). Fewer women than men know other entrepreneurs and believe they have sufficient skills to run a business. This suggests that men are more confident in their abilities than women and also have better business networks.

As women become increasingly active in the workforce, the number starting their own business is also growing. Despite advances in equality legislation and pay, female earnings still lag behind men's and entrepreneurship offers the potential for increased earnings. Female entrepreneurs can also help alleviate poverty and provide better education and nutrition for their children.

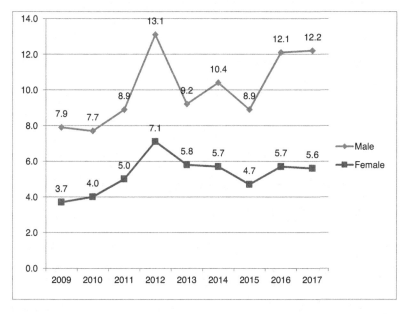

Figure 6.1 Male and female entrepreneurs from 2009 to 2017

Source: Adapted from the Rose Review (2019:33)

Table 6.1 Barriers for female entrepreneurs to start a business

Access to funding	Female entrepreneurs start a business with less capital than men
Family responsibilities	Women are usually the primary carers for children and the elderly
Risk awareness	Females tend to be more concerned about the risks than men
Confidence	Women tend to have less confidence about their managerial skills
Networks	Female entrepreneurs are less likely to know another entrepreneur

GEM women's report

There is evidence that the gender gap is closing and Kelley et al. (2017) found that there had been a 6% reduction in the gender gap for total entrepreneurial activity. Women only participate at a level equal to men in two

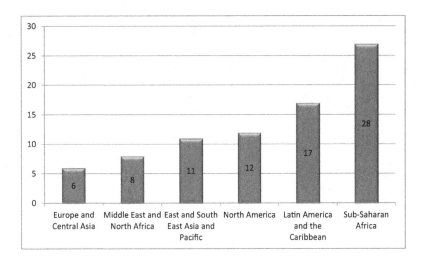

Figure 6.2 Regional Averages for Female Total Entrepreneurial Activity (as a % age of the Female Population Aged 18–64)

Source: Kelley et al. (2017:18)

regions of the world, Asia and Latin America, and they are more likely to be driven by necessity than men. However, the majority of women are motivated by opportunity. Better job opportunities for women as economies develop may mean that they are less likely to start a business. However, despite lower entrepreneurial participation in developed countries, women owned businesses are more likely to survive.

Kelley et al. (2017) found that, despite the increasing levels of female participation in entrepreneurship, there were still some areas of concern. The first one was that women were 20% more likely to be necessity-driven than men. The second concern was that there was a disconnection between the number of women who wanted to start a business and those who succeeded in doing so. This would indicate that there are still some additional hurdles for women to starting a business. For those who did start a business, their growth aspirations were lower than for men. In addition, the rate of business discontinuance was higher for women than for men.

Men and women are more likely to become entrepreneurs at a similar age, with more women starting a business in the 25–24 and 35–44 age ranges. In Europe, female entrepreneurs are 22% more likely to have a college degree than male entrepreneurs and in North America, 84% of women entrepreneurs have post-secondary-education qualifications (Kelley et al. 2017). Approximately 10% of the women did not employ anyone else and had no intention of taking on employees in the next five years. Europe had the highest proportion of women working on their own, with North America having the lowest. Women in the US are twice as likely to be entrepreneurially active as in the UK and 30% of all US businesses are majority female owned. The number of women-owned businesses is growing at twice the rate of all US firms.

The lowest growth intentions were found in Latin America, with female expectations of growth at 60% of the males. In some countries, such as Saudi Arabia, females have more growth expectations. Levels of innovation were high, with women 5% more likely than men to have innovative products and services. Women were 16% more likely to start businesses in the wholesale/retail sector and only 2% in the ICT sector. Female entrepreneurs are less likely to invest in business than men and are less likely to know an entrepreneur in developed economies.

More than 163 million women entrepreneurs were starting or running new businesses in 67 economies in 2016 (GEM, 2017). In every single economy in the study, women have lower capabilities perceptions than men. Women also have a greater fear of failure.

Women are nearly five times more likely to mention family reasons for becoming self-employed than men. Men are more likely to say that the reason to start a business is to 'make money.' On average, 30% of self-employed women and 8% of men work at home. Eight percent of women want to start a business, compared with 13% of men. More than half of women chose to start their businesses part-time, compared to 12% of men. Women are more likely to start their businesses undercapitalised, which may lead to lower profits and growth prospects.

Underperformance

There have been some criticisms of the underperformance approach to female entrepreneurship, i.e., their performance relative to male entrepreneurs (Ahl, 2006). Some studies have looked at the structural barriers to female entrepreneurship, such as access to finance and networks, and there is the assumption that, if these barriers were removed, women would achieve the same as men. The criticisms are based on the fact that economic growth is measured in a very narrow way and that businesses run by female entrepreneurs are more likely to survive. One of the reasons given for the underperformance is that women start businesses in the retail and service industries where there is strong competition, which put pressure on profits because of the low barriers to entry.

The need for flexibility because of family responsibilities, it is argued, is not only relevant for women. In addition, having family responsibilities does not appear to affect growth or the numbers of hours worked in the business. The second issue, the glass ceiling, was introduced in the 1980s as a result of women failing to be promoted to the top levels of management. The assumption, then, is that women are pushed into entrepreneurship because they lack the management and knowledge gained through experience. However, many male entrepreneurs start a business with low levels of education and experience of top management in organisations. It is possible, however, that male entrepreneurs have higher levels of self-confidence in their management abilities.

Case study: Laura Ashley

Laura Ashley is a well-known brand on the high street and in the retail centres of major towns and cities in the UK. The company also has shops in Europe, North America and the Far East. The business was originally founded by Laura Ashley in her kitchen in London. She printed the material herself on a homemade press made by her husband, Bernard. Laura was born in Wales, and, as soon as the business became established, she moved to Powys and set up a manufacturing unit in Carno near Newtown. Laura designed and printed the fabric and made the clothes that she, herself, wanted to wear. She would go to the Victoria and Albert museum in London to look at Victorian designs of flowers and would base her designs on small, pretty florals. Initially, these were printed in two colours to keep the costs down. Laura would use the same fabric for clothes and soft furnishings. Despite her fame and success, however, she did not give up on her core values and based her business on her fundamental philosophies. Laura Ashley wanted everyone to enjoy her style of dressing and home furnishings, whether they lived in a cottage or a stately home.

The business grew and Laura Ashley soon opened shops in other countries. One of the keys to her success was the decision to vertically integrate the manufacturing process. The company employed over 4,000 people in mid Wales and plans were made to float the company on the stock exchange. Six months before the floatation, Laura Ashley fell down the stairs and died from a head injury a few weeks later. Laura Ashley's importance as a female entrepreneur is considerable. She brought a caring approach to looking after employees and creating employment in mid Wales was an important part of her strategy. After her death, the head office was moved to London and the number of people employed in mid Wales gradually fell. Laura Ashley is now owned by a Malaysian company, MUI Asia Limited. The strategy in more recent years has been to focus on home furnishing, as these have been more profitable. Some of the soft furnishings, such as curtains, are still manufactured in mid Wales. Laura Ashley created employment in an area where there was little alternative employment and she was a role model for other female entrepreneurs.

For discussion

1 How did Laura Ashley create her style? How important was the vertical integration?
2 Why did the company lose direction after she died?

Exercise

• Identify the approach taken by Laura Ashley that illustrates the importance of supporting female entrepreneurs.

Finance for female entrepreneurs

Research has also shown that women face additional problems when trying to raise funding and men are more likely to use external funding for their businesses than female entrepreneurs. Brush et al. (2004) found that women invested less in their businesses than men because they did not have the same level of financial resources available. One of the reasons for this is that women in employment earn, on average, 70% of the male average wages.

Sources of finance are becoming more accessible for women. Generally, women still tend to rely on more accessible sources of finance, such as credit cards, and are generally more reluctant to seek bank financing than men. However, when women choose to seek bank finance, the owner's credit risk and prospects are more important than gender. Women generally have lower levels of savings to start their business and rely on friends and family to help them get started. Women who do actually start a business have a high chance of success and can earn more than females in full-time employment. Women also often take a more cautious approach to raising finance.

Venture capitalists usually concentrate on one industry sector, such as IT, biotechnology, software, etc. The majority of women starting a business in these sectors is very low, as they generally tend to focus on service industries, although the number of women starting a technology-based business is growing. There are, of course, many examples of women who have grown a retail business, such as Laura Ashley and Laura Tenison, but they did develop their own products. According to Brush et al. (2004:226), the most highly qualified women still find it difficult to raise venture capital because they 'don't know the right people and don't know the ropes.'

Characteristics of female entrepreneurs

The perceptions about women's role at work and in business may be influenced by their education, society, the media, their families and their experiences. Even if both parents work, the female is more likely to take care of childcare, cooking and housework whereas the male is more likely to take care of maintenance and repairs. Education also plays a role in developing gender stereotypes in that the percentage of women studying science and technology is lower than for men.

The main reasons given by women for starting a business (Brush et al., 2004:80) were learning and personal achievement, with flexibility and economic reasons less important. They also found in a survey of 800 nascent entrepreneurs that 24% of the male respondents wanted to have a business as large as possible, but only 15% of the women reported the same.

Women's businesses have a higher churn rate (more start-ups and closures) and women are more likely to attribute closure to 'business failure' and cite 'personal reasons.'

Despite making great strides in the workplace and in equal-opportunities legislation, female earnings are still only 70% of the male equivalent. Also, fewer women reach the higher level of management and are generally under-represented at board level. One way of avoiding the glass ceiling in the workplace is to become an entrepreneur and an increasing number of women have taken this route in the last few years.

Innovation

The proportion of women registering patents worldwide increased from 6.8% to 12% between 1998 and 2017. There was also an increase in the number of patents where women were amongst the inventors increased to 21% from 12%

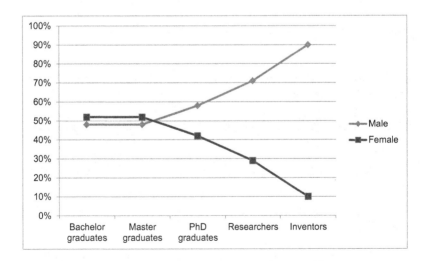

Figure 6.3 The percentages of male and females in higher education, research and inventors

Source: Adapted from IPO (2019:6)

over the same period. The areas with the most participation by women were pharmaceuticals, biotechnology and organic chemistry.

Figure 6.2 (IPO, 2019) shows the number of men and women studying STEM (science, technology, engineering and mathematics) subjects who then went on to careers as researchers and inventors. The drop in the number of women is described as the 'leaky pipeline' and shows the low number registering patents. Up until 1965, the patents registered by females was between 2% to 3% of the total; there was a considerable increase to 12.7% by 2017. In addition, one in five patent applications in 2017 had at least one female inventor. Interestingly, 80% of all female teams registering a patent had two persons, whereas only 50% of the male teams had two persons. Female inventions are also more likely to take place in higher education, possibly as a result of postgraduate study, rather than in industry (IPO, 2019).

Case study: Laura Tenison, JoJo Maman Bebe

JoJo Maman Bebe is one of the leading specialist retailers in the UK for maternity and baby clothes and accessories. Laura Tenison started the business in 1993 and now has a thriving online presence, catalogue and mail order business as well as a chain of shops in the UK. Following the tradition of Laura Ashley, she still designs the clothes herself. The business expanded rapidly and, at one stage, was opening new shops each year.

Laura Tenison won the Veuve Cliquot Business Woman of the Year award in 2010 for building up the company to a £21 million turnover and 280 employees and for embedding a sense of social responsibility into the company. She was awarded an MBE for service to business in 2004 for her success in founding and growing JoJo Maman Bebe in Newport, South Wales.

Laura Tenison had been running a property business in France when she was involved in a car accident. She had sold the business and wanted to go back to the UK, as she had recently got married. When she was in hospital in France she met a young mother who was seriously ill and wanted to buy clothes for her children from her hospital bed. Laura loved the French style of dressing both for children and pregnant women and designed her first collection based on the Breton nautical style.

JoJo Maman Bebe is based on a strong ethical approach to business. Some of the staff have been with Laura since she started and she feels that looking after her staff is important. She started a charity to help disadvantaged children in Mozambique and Laura cycled from the design office in Newport, South Wales to London to raise money for the charity. One of the reasons for starting the charity was to involve the staff in helping people in Africa and to see people worse off than themselves and living in poverty.

For discussion

1   What were the motivations for JoJo Maman Bebe to have its own charity?
2   Discuss why female entrepreneurs may be more aware of the need to look after their staff.

Exercise

•   Identify other charities set up by female entrepreneurs.

Networks

Networks can provide entrepreneurs with access to a wider range of resources than are available from family and friends. This may be very important, for example, when looking for external funds, especially business angel or venture capital financing. Developing links with suppliers and customers is an important part of networks, and it's important to build a good relationship with them. Traditionally, business networks have been largely seen as male dominated and female participation was not encouraged. However, this situation may be changing as the numbers of female-owned businesses has grown, and the increased participation of women in networks. Brush et al. (2004) found that networks and social capital and the ability to use them effectively were important in making sure the financial, human and technological resources were available. Women tend to associate with close links such as family and friends, and business networks are seen as providing emotional and social support, whereas men tend to join networks for business purposes.

Ethnic minority entrepreneurs

Ethnic minority entrepreneurs can also make an important contribution to the economy. There is evidence that some groups find it more difficult to raise finance. This may, of course, depend on the assessment of the risk. Some groups are more entrepreneurial than others. For example, women of mixed ethnicity are two-and-a-half times more entrepreneurial than white women. The predominant source of finance for ethnic groups is 'friends and family.' For example, finance for Pakistani groups from friends and family is over 90%.

There has been a growing awareness of the importance of diversity in entrepreneurship and the contribution minority entrepreneurs can make to the economy. One of the questions has been as to why some of these groups have lower participation in entrepreneurship. In response to these concerns, the UK government has developed policies to address the additional hurdles that female and minority entrepreneurs may face.

There is some evidence to show that people who are displaced are more likely to start a business in their new home. The self-employment rate for the UK population as a whole is 15% and all groups have seen an increase between 2011 and 2017. There are significant differences in entrepreneurial activity between ethnic minority groups, and 24% of Pakistani and Bangladeshi people are self-employed. People of African-Caribbean origin have seen a significant increase in self-employment from 8% in 2011 to 12.8% in 2017, showing high levels of entrepreneurial aspirations. The levels for Indian and mixed-race people are 12.8% and 13.7%, respectively, showing a slightly lower self-employment than the population as a whole (Gov.uk, 2018).

Some ethnic groups are concentrated in particular sectors. The Chinese, for example, are more likely to have businesses in distribution, hotels and restaurants. Ethnic minority businesses also tend to concentrate on supplying minority businesses and often trade with members their own ethnic groups. This concentration of activity within the ethnic group offers a focus, but may also constrain growth as a result of overdependence on one market.

Case study: Cobra Beer

Cobra Beer was founded by Karan Bilimora, who identified a niche market. Although his parents wanted him to be an accountant, he decided to set up his own business and decided to make a less fizzy beer to be drunk with a curry. Bilimora would save costs by delivering the crates of beer himself to Indian restaurants. By targeting the ethnic minority market, Cobra Beer became well established in its niche market. It was a niche that none of the big brewers had targeted, as it was considered too niche. Bilimora concentrated on developing the brand and priced the beer at the top end of the market. The beer was initially brewed in India, but after problems with the quality, the production was moved to the UK. Although the first few years were difficult, he never thought of giving up, but his partner, Arjun Reddy, decided to return to India. Bilimora sold shares in the company to raise £500,000. The company got into financial difficulties and Molson Coors bought a controlling interest in June 2011.

For discussion

1   What were the benefits of targeting a niche market such as Indian restaurants?
2   Discuss the importance of maintaining high quality at the top end of the market.

Exercise

•   Identify other products that could be targeted at a similar niche market.

Other under-represented groups

Other under-represented and disadvantaged groups include those in inner cities and rural areas, refugees, the disabled, the mentally handicapped and ex-offenders. Some of these groups, such as ex-offenders, may find it difficult to obtain employment, and self-employment enables them to earn a living and make a contribution to the economy. Social enterprises can employ ex-offenders and the mentally handicapped and can also make a contribution to the economy and some have been set up for this purpose.

Conclusion

The contribution that previously under-represented groups can make to economic prosperity is now recognised and there is now a greater understanding of some of the hurdles that they may face in trying to set up their own business. Females are particularly under-represented as business owners, and even when they do start a business, their earnings and number of employees are lower than male entrepreneurs. Women are also less likely to enter into high-growth, high-technology businesses. There are now many initiatives, support and training programmes to help women getting into business. There are many other issues to consider when dealing with groups that are under-achieving with regard to setting up and growing a business.

References

Ahl, H. (2006). Why research on women entrepreneurs needs new directions. *Entrepreneurship Theory and Practice*, *30*(5), 595–621.

Brush, C., Carter, N. M., Gatewood, E., Greene, P. G., & Hart, M. M. (2004). *Clearing the Hurdles: Women building high growth businesses*. London: Financial Times Prentice Hall.

Elam, A.B., Brush, C.G, Greene, P. G., Baumer, B. Dean, M. and Havlov, R., (2019). 'Global Entrepreneurship Monitor: 2018/2019 Women's Entrepreneurship Report'. Retrieved from www.gemconsortium.com

Gov.uk (2018). *Ethnicity facts and figures*. Retrieved October 18, 2019, from www. ethnicity-facts-figures.service.gov.uk/workforce-and-business/business-and-self-employment/self-employment/latest

IPO (2019). *Gender profiles in worldwide patenting: An analysis of female inventorship* (2019 ed.). Newport: Intellectual Property Office.

Kelley, D.J., Brush, C.G., Greene, P.G. and Litovsky, Y., (2011). 'Global Entrepreneurship (GEM): Women's Report'. Babson Park. Babson College. retrieved from www.gemconsortium.com

Kelley, D. J., Baumer, B. S., Brush, C., Greene, P. G., Mahdavi, M., Cole, M. M. M., ... Heavlow, R. (2017). Women's entrepreneurship 2016/2017 report. *Global Entrepreneurship Research Association*. Retrieved from http://gemconsortium.org

Rose Review (2019). The Alison Rose Review of female entrepreneurship. *GOV. UK*. Retrieved October 15, 2019, from www.gov.uk/government/publications/the-alison-rose-review-of-female-entrepreneurship

7 Entrepreneurial strategies

Summary

Entrepreneurial strategies include growing, holding and harvesting the business. Porter's (1985) generic strategies include cost leadership, differentiation or focus on a target market. The entrepreneur's role at each stage of business growth changes from hands-on direct management to delegation and, eventually, watchdog. Entrepreneurial marketing strategies are often based on the entrepreneur's personal networking skills, word-of-mouth recommendations and focus on a niche market. Financing the business includes bootstrapping, i.e., starting a business with very little money, debt or equity finance, which is money invested for a share of the profits. Managing the finances can be difficult, especially in the early stages when cash-flow is likely to be negative. A small increase in price can have a significant effect on profits. A harvesting strategy can be either a sale of all or part of the business, including a stock market flotation. Turnaround strategies can include contraction, survival or growth by increasing sales and improving profitability.

Entrepreneurial strategies

A strategy is a long-term plan for the business. Entrepreneurial strategies will have a different focus from large organisations due to the availability of resources. Strategies can be planned or emergent, i.e., a combination of a planned strategy and events that have shaped a change in direction. In reality, planned strategies will have to be adapted and one of the advantages of an entrepreneurial strategy is that it can be modified at short notice. The entrepreneur will have a vision in order to provide the direction for the business and this will be communicated to stakeholders including employees and investors.

Porter's generic strategy

Porter (1985) outlined the competitive pressure on firms and has identified the areas to avoid. These five forces will increase the pressure on profits. For example, strong customers can push the prices down and powerful suppliers can charge high prices. Intense competition in the industry will push prices down and affect profitability. Substitute products can also put a ceiling on the price than can be charged for a product or service. Low barriers to entry can make it easy for new entrants into the market and this can also increase competition and affect profits. The key is to avoid these situations when starting a business.

1   Intense competition in the industry
2   Substitute products
3   Strong suppliers
4   Powerful customers
5   Threat of new entry

According to Porter (1980), there are three generic strategies that a business can adopt (Figure 7.1). The first, overall cost leadership, is being cheaper as a result of economies of scale. Unless sufficient funds are available for a major capital investment, then this option is unlikely to be attractive for new businesses. A differentiation strategy is based on making the product or service different,

Figure 7.1 Porter's generic strategies

and ensuring good quality and design. Focusing on the target market is also more manageable for a new business and also can have high margins. These two strategies can be merged so that a business can differentiate the product or service and focus on a target segment.

Growth strategies

Some entrepreneurs will start a business with a growth strategy in mind from the beginning. However, a growth strategy will require considerable investment and high levels of effort and perseverance on the part of the entrepreneur (Douglas, 2013). Only a very small percentage of businesses will grow to be large ones. The main prerequisite for growth are the skills and aspirations of the entrepreneur.

Once a business is established, it will go through various stages of growth (Table 7.1). The first stage is existence, when the company is formed and it starts trading. The next stage is survival, when the entrepreneur manages to keep the company going and pay the bills. Many businesses get stuck in this survival mode and may stay there for months or even years. The success stage is reached when the business gets out of the survival stage and starts marking profits regularly. Take-off can then be achieved into the high growth stage and the business may then reach maturity.

There are crisis points at each stage of growth and the business can face problems as it grows. The first six months may be the most difficult as the business faces the valley of death. Entrepreneurs often underestimate the time and money that is necessary to start a business and get sufficient sales to survive. Once the business is in survival stage, then cash flow can cause

Table 7.1 Entrepreneur's role at the stages of business growth

Stage of growth	Entrepreneur's management role	Management style	Organisational Structure
Existence	Direct supervision	Entrepreneurial individualistic	Unstructured
Survival	Supervised supervision	Entrepreneurial administrative	Simple
Growth	Delegation and co-ordination	Entrepreneurial co-ordination	Functional centralised
Expansion	Decentralised	Professional administrative	Functional decentralised
Maturity	Decentralised	Watchdog	Decentralised functional/product

Source: Adapted from Lewis and Churchill (1983)

a crisis if there isn't enough money to pay the bills. Rapid growth can cause its own problems, as cash flow may not keep up with the requirements of the business. When the business reaches success and take-off, the entrepreneur needs to keep developing the product and services and failure to innovate at this stage can lead to a decline in sales.

As the business grows, entrepreneurs need to create structures and systems that can help them grow the business. The management will also change as the business grows and the entrepreneur will need to develop new skills or appoint people with the relevant skills and abilities.

The ability to grow a business beyond what the entrepreneur can manage personally depends on their skills and characteristics as well as their aspirations. In the initial stages, the entrepreneurs do everything themselves and will play different roles within the business. The business itself will be unstructured but, as it grows, an organisational structure will be developed, probably in the different functions such as financial, production and marketing. As the number of employees increase, then supervision will change from direct supervision by the entrepreneur to delegation and, finally, to stepping back and acting as a watchdog. There are examples of where the founding entrepreneurs have stepped back only to be called in at a later date when the business is facing some challenges.

Successful entrepreneurs are able to create a team to help them manage the business. However, this may not be easy for entrepreneurs, as they have to acknowledge that they may not have all the necessary skills themselves. In addition, delegation may also be difficult, as entrepreneurs will have to give up an element of control.

Case study: Easygroup

The Easygroup of companies was established by Stelio Haji-Ioannou following the floatation of Easyjet on the stock exchange in 2000. The strategy for Easyjet was based on a case study of Southwest Airlines that Stelios had studied at university. During the IPO process, Stelios decided to keep the 'Easy' brand in order to licence it out to other companies, including Easyjet. The strategy for Easyjet itself was based on low overheads and providing value for money and this has been extended to other businesses, such as Easycar and Easymoney. One of the ways that Southwest Airlines was able to keep its costs low was by using the same type of jet and short flights, and this is the strategy that Stelios adopted for Easyjet. This enables Easyjet to make numerous flights in one day with quick turnarounds, which helps to reduce costs. Easyjet was able to keep its costs low was by direct booking by the customers and the company was an early adopter of online booking. Previously, customers would book through travel agents and this new strategy was soon copied by the competitors.

For discussion

1 Discuss the approach taken by Easygroup's strategy.
2 What is the strategic importance of targeting the 'many' rather than the 'few'?

Exercise

• Identify the entrepreneurial aspects of Stelio Hajo-Ioannou's strategy. Has this strategy been inspired by other entrepreneurs?

Networks

One of the most important elements for the success of a new business and for innovation is external networks. These can provide sources of information and support for the entrepreneur. The advantage of external networks for the entrepreneur is that they can access resources that they would not otherwise be able to afford, especially in the early stages. One of the reasons for the success of Silicon Valley is that firms can share resources, including staff, and provide inspiration and support. Social capital is important for the entrepreneur to develop access to financing, for example.

Entrepreneurial marketing strategies

Entrepreneurial marketing strategies are often driven by a low or nonexistent marketing budget and/or the personality and approach of the entrepreneur Figure 7.2. Entrepreneurs often find themselves focusing on other aspects of the

Figure 7.2 Entrepreneurial marketing strategies

business because of scarce resources and it's difficult for them to focus on marketing. The entrepreneurs will, therefore, tend to fall back on their own networking and relationship building skills.

Having a marketing strategy is very important in a new and growing business. Marketing with few resources available has to be very innovative. Many businesses fail because of insufficient sales.

Entrepreneurs will control all aspects of the business, including the marketing. The business will reflect the entrepreneur's personality and values and this is reflected in the branding and marketing. One of the advantages that the entrepreneur has is that they can react quickly to customers and changes in the market.

The entrepreneurial approach to market research, especially in the early stages of the business, is by asking their customers directly, and collecting information on a daily basis. Entrepreneurs usually prefer informal market research. This may be because of cost implications. They also collect information from networks of suppliers, professional advisors and other businesses as well as from wider sources. This approach to market research is informal but can be quite effective.

Entrepreneurs usually adopt a hands-on, face-to-face approach to marketing. They develop relationships with their customers and this can give them a competitive edge over larger firms. The more distinctive the competitive advantages are, the more the price can be increased. However, many smaller firms compete only on price because they cannot differentiate their products or services efficiently.

The entrepreneurial personality has a significant impact on all aspects of the management of a small firm, especially marketing. Entrepreneurs will have to manage all aspects of the business initially and this includes all elements of marketing such as sales, advertising, customer relationships, etc. Entrepreneurs often rely on informal marketing techniques such as word-of-mouth recommendation. A marketing approach is a planned process of finding out customer needs and developing products and services to meet these needs. The entrepreneurial approach, on the other handed, is often unplanned and informal.

The entrepreneurial approach to marketing is, however, focused on developing customer relationships. Customer recommendations are considered to be very important by entrepreneurs, and Stokes (2000) found that they would devote considerable time to ensuring that customers are satisfied and will recommend the business to others.

Word-of-mouth marketing is very important for the small business and can have a significant influence on customers' purchasing behaviour. For the entrepreneurs, this a relatively low-cost approach and provides the opportunity to build up the business slowly. However, it can have disadvantages in that the entrepreneur cannot control the message. Some entrepreneurs may provide incentives for word-of-mouth recommendations.

As the business grows, the owner-manager of a small business will start to adopt more formal marketing strategies. However, in the early stages of development, and depending on the type of business, there will probably be an over-reliance on a small group of customers. If some of these customers are lost, then this can have a significant adverse effect on the business.

Market research

Many entrepreneurs have to adopt an innovative approach to market research and one of the easiest ways is to ask the customers or potential customers face-to-face. However, this may give a biased result and other approaches may give a more informed result.

Case study: Innocent Drinks

Richard Reed, Adam Balon and Jon Wright founded Innocent Drinks in 1998. The three had been friends at Cambridge University where they had often talked about starting a business. When they left Cambridge, all three of them got jobs, one in advertising and two in management consulting. Four years later they went on a snowboarding holiday and decided to become entrepreneurs. They wanted something that would appeal to people like them and decided that it would be something that was good for them. They thought of a fruit smoothie as a way of eating more fruit.

In 1998, after trying out recipes on their friends, they invested £500 in buying fruit to make smoothies to take to a small music festival in London. They put up a big sign above two dustbins asking if they thought they should give up their jobs to make smoothies. One of the dustbins had YES on it and the other had NO (Figure 7.3). At the end of the weekend, the YES bin was full and they resigned from their jobs the next day.

The name Innocent came from wanting to show that it was pure fruit. From the beginning, the three founders were determined a run a business where the image and the product were the same. The company's headquarters is called Fruit Towers and in the early years an Innocent smoothie came with a small booklet outlining the company's ethos.

Having failed to raise venture capital, the founders of Innocent wrote to their friends asking if they knew anyone rich who wanted to invest in their business. Maurice Pinto, an American businessman, had listened to their pitch at a formal presentation to his venture capital fund. The venture capital fund turned them down, but Pinto decided to invest his own money and gave them a loan of £250,000.

Figure 7.3 Innocent's market research

The company spent very little on advertising and decided on distributing the smoothies and growing the business slowly. One aspect of developing the brand was that the founders felt that if the company was called Innocent, they had a responsibility to ensure that their business reflected innocence. By 2003, the business had 30% of the market and was valued at £50 million. The market itself was growing quickly. Coca-Cola bought 18% of the business in 2009 for £30 million and a year later paid £65 million for 58%.

Discussion questions

1   The founders of Innocent Drinks used a very simple approach to market research. Discuss whether this would be suitable for other types of businesses.
2   The culture developed by Innocent to create the brand was very innovative. Describe how they created the brand image.

Exercise

•   Outline a marketing strategy for a new business and outline informal market research that could be carried out.

Branding

Although branding is often seen as something for large organisations, it is also very important for a new venture. A successful brand can differentiate a product or service that will make it easier to gain customer loyalty. Brands can be an asset to the business and have a value if it is sold.

Table 7.2 Creating a successful brand

Quality	It's important to maintain the quality in order to justify the higher price
Excellent service	This is more difficult for competitors to copy than the product or service
Innovation	The first product or service that enters the market will be in the customer's minds
Differentiation	This encourages customer loyalty and enables higher prices to be charged

Table 7.3 Different aspects of branding

Name	*What it's called*
Logo	A symbol or a form of writing
Trademark	Signs and words which can be legally protected

In order to create a successful brand, there is also a need to ensure the aspects of the business shown in Table 7.2.

One of the advantages of creating a brand is that it can create a perception of quality. This can give the entrepreneur increased bargaining power with customers and suppliers. It can also enable the entrepreneur to charge higher prices for the product or service. Another important advantage is the option to market new products or services under the same brand name, e.g., Virgin.

Business name

The business name can be used for branding (Table 7.3). Some entrepreneurs name the business after their own surname and/or their initials and there are many examples where this has been successful, e.g., Cadbury, JCB, etc. The name can also be used to describe the service to be offered or some other aspect of the business.

Brand extension

A successful brand can be used to launch other products or services. Richard Branson has done this very successfully with the Virgin brand, which has been used for a range of products including music and airlines. It is easier to launch a new product or service using an established brand. Customers are already aware of the brand and entrepreneurs can, therefore, spend less on promotion. Using an existing brand to promote a new product or service can have disadvantages. If the new product or service is unsuccessful, then this can have a detrimental effect on the brand.

Bootstrapping

According to Bhide (1992), many entrepreneurs waste time and money looking for external financing, especially in the early stages of the business. Raising a lot of money requires considerable effort, time and resources and a very comprehensive and detailed business plan. Many successful businesses have started with very little money. External equity finance is very difficult and venture capitalists only fund a very low percentage of businesses. Although most books and articles are focused on raising money for a new business, entrepreneurs need to ask themselves if it's absolutely necessary.

Although some businesses need a large amount of external finance to get started, especially when there is a large upfront investment in infrastructure, the majority of businesses are started with very little. The entrepreneurs' own savings, credit cards, second mortgages, redundancy, etc., can all be used to start a business. The criteria for external funding from venture capitalists are quite narrow and there is often a gap between what their requirements are and what the entrepreneur has to offer. Often the entrepreneur has to target a niche market that may not be of interest to external investors because of the lack of potential to expand. On the other hand, if the business is successful in raising finance it can lead to problems, as the entrepreneur may lose the ability to make decisions without consulting the investors. The investors will want the entrepreneur to stick to the business plan and this may also cause problems when new opportunities arise and inhibit the entrepreneurial approach.

Starting a business with limited funds needs a different strategy. This includes:

1   Get operational quickly
2   Look for break-even, cash-generating projects
3   Offer high-value products or services that sustain direct personal selling
4   Forget about the crack team
5   Keep growth in check
6   Focus on cash, not profits, market share or anything else
7   Cultivate banks before the business become credit worthy

Adapted from Bhide (1992)

According to Bhide (1992), the key is to get operational quickly in order to generate cash flow. This can be done by starting with a copycat idea, as this can save time and effort, including market research and development. Once the business has been started and is generating a positive cash flow, then other opportunities can be developed. Entrepreneurs often have good selling skills and using their enthusiasm and commitment to sell high-value products or services may overcome customer inertia.

Case study: Apple Computers

When Steve Jobs and Steve Wozniak started Apple Computers, they used the garage in Steve Jobs' home. Jobs got an order for 50 computers at $500 each. He arranged a small loan from friends and bought $15,000 of parts on 30 days' credit. The customer was not happy with the delivery, as they were only partially assembled, but he paid the bill and Jobs was able to pay his suppliers. They made $8,000 and were able to survive and later expand.

For discussion

1 How important was the purchase of parts on credit for Steve Jobs and Steve Wozniak?
2 What were the other steps that they took to keep the costs down?

Exercise

• What other products could be assembled within the 30 days' credit and delivered to customers?

Equity finance

Equity finance can be the entrepreneur's own funds, retained profits or money invested by others. Equity finance can be provided by institutional equity firms or business angels. Venture capitalists usually target a particular sector such as high technology or biotechnology, or a stage of the business such as expansion or management buy-outs. Interest is not paid, but the investors have an equity share in the business. Equity investors are entitled to a share of the profits in the form of dividends. However, many investors in small firms are looking for capital growth.

Since the *Dragons' Den* television series started, equity finance has had an increased profile. However, it is only suitable for high-growth firms with potential to make profits and returns for the investors. In reality, only a very small percentage of new firms obtain equity funding. There are different types of equity capital available (Table 7.4). Private equity is the term that covers the industry as a whole, including management buy-outs and expansion capital, whereas venture capital usually covers start-ups and early stages of investment.

Various methods can be used to value a business for equity investment, but it's usually based on profits. Investors may prefer staged investments, as this lowers the risk. Entrepreneurs need to maintain good relationships with their investors, as they may need further investment over time.

Table 7.4 Types of equity finance

Equity capital	Money invested for a share of the business
Private equity	Equity finance invested in private companies
Venture capital	Money invested in new or growing businesses
Business angels	High net worth individuals who invest new and growing businesses
Family and friends	Family and friends are usually the first to invest
Crowdfunding	Groups of investors usually via the internet

Business angels

Business angels can fill the finance gap between family and friends and venture capital. They are private investors who buy a share in an unquoted company with no family connections. The business angels can provide more than financial support, in that they can also offer management expertise. They may have built up a successful business themselves and can provide support for entrepreneurs. They will usually only invest in a few companies, either in their specialist area or in a geographical region. Although the main motivation is capital gain, they may also want to be involved in the business as nonexecutive directors. The business angels may also be willing to invest in early-stage, riskier businesses. As they bring in their expertise, they can be a valuable addition to the management team and recipient firms are likely to grow much faster.

Crowdfunding

There has been a considerable growth in crowdfunding for business purposes due to the ease of raising money through the internet. Entrepreneurs can pitch the idea on the internet and the idea is that large numbers of people can invest small amounts of money. Investors can have a share in the business or other benefits, such as a prototype product or a service. With crowdfunding, the investment will only go ahead if all the money is raised. Loans are also available via crowdfunding sites, mainly peer-to-peer lending.

UK government equity funding

Enterprise Capital Funds are a combination of private and public money to provide equity finance in high growth businesses. The British Business Bank invests alongside private sector funds, so that they can invest in sectors that would be too small for the venture capital institutions. The rationale for this government support is the 'equity gap.' The maximum that can be invested is £5 million and the business must meet the EU definition of a SME. The company must have been trading for seven years and the investment must not be higher than 50% of its annual turnover for the preceding five years. There are other regional sources of venture capital, e.g., the Development Bank of Wales.

Franchising

Franchising can provide a relatively low-cost way of expanding the business for entrepreneurs who have developed a concept and a brand and want to expand at a faster rate than they would be able to finance themselves. Once the entrepreneur has established that the business concept works and is profitable, then this can be franchised, i.e., the right to operate it in other geographical locations. There has been a significant increase in the number of franchising businesses in recent years, especially in retail and fast food outlets. In some industries, e.g., restaurants, a considerable investment is required for each outlet. By using the franchise model, the entrepreneur can expand more quickly. The rapid expansion then increases market share, which can lead to high profitability.

The franchisor develops the business concept, including the service delivery system, which is the key to successful franchising. Choosing the franchisees is important and many franchisors will specify the kind of person they are looking for and how much capital they will need to invest. The relationship between the franchisee and the franchisor is important.

Managing the finances

Entrepreneurs are willing to take the risk of setting up their own business. This means that they will manage the business and put in the long hours necessary to develop their own products or services. This attitude to risk may have an effect on the financial management of the business. The entrepreneur will also probably have a high proportion of their assets tied up in the business and, because the business itself has a high risk, then this is a risky portfolio. Even if the business has limited liability, in practice lenders will often ask entrepreneurs to put up a personal guarantee or personal assets as security for a loan.

Why do new businesses have cash flow issues? If there isn't enough money to pay the staff and suppliers before receiving payment for the customers, there will be a cash flow crisis. There may be overoptimism on the part of the entrepreneur, especially in sales and profit projections, which can lead to discrepancies in the cash flow projections. This can lead to problems with banks and other lenders, who may make demands for more information. The banks may also charge more for loans and overdrafts, which can create more financial pressure. The overoptimism on the part of the entrepreneurs can also lead to other problems, such as overinvestment in fixed assets, which can also have an adverse effect on cash flow. One of the essential tasks for the entrepreneur, especially in the early stages of the business, is to ensure that there is sufficient cash available to pay the bills.

The costs of running the business may also be higher than anticipated. In a new business, the relationships with suppliers are infrequent and informal and they cannot benefit from economies of scale. The entrepreneur does, however, have flexibility in how much money they take out of the business. They will often delay paying themselves in the early days in order to improve cash flow.

Cash flow is often an issue in the first few months of a business, as entrepreneurs may have underestimated the time it takes to get new customers. It may take several months to generate sufficient income to cover the costs. These costs still have to be paid, even if there are very few sales. The cash flow can be negative for the first few months and, until sales pick up, and this can have severe consequences on a new business. The cash is going out quickly and the business needs to generate enough sales to get out of the downwards spiral. If the situation deteriorates, then the business may be unable to survive. If it does survive, it may have to carry the debt incurred during this time, which will cost more money to service.

If there is a cash-flow crisis, then the entrepreneur can take steps to raise additional cash in the short term. A factoring company, for example, can lend up to 80% of the value of the firm's invoices. There is a cost, but the factoring companies also provide advice on credit risk and insurance against bad debts. Other ideas include invoice discounting, offering a discount for prompt payment, and grants and other government support. For the longer term, more accurate budgeting, reducing mistakes and providing incentives for profits rather than sales may help. If there is a real cash crunch, then the entrepreneur can negotiate with the banks and creditors and cut costs, including staff, if necessary.

Profits

One of the other issues that entrepreneurs may face is understanding the difference between cash flow and profits. A business can be very profitable but still have a cash flow crisis, with insufficient money in the bank to pay wages and the bills. Profits are the difference between the income that the business earns and all the costs over a period of time.

Many small firms feel that they have to charge low prices to attract customers. They will often use a cost plus method of pricing (Table 7.5). This method is to take the total cost of a product and divide by the number of units. This

Table 7.5 Pricing strategies

Costs	What the price should be to cover the costs
Market	What the customers will pay
Profits	What price is needed to make the projected profits
Mark-up	Retailers and wholesalers work on a mark-up of the original price

approach may not take into account fixed costs. One of the ways of working out pricing is by working out the contribution margin. For example, a small increase in price may have a significant positive effect on profits.

The 80/20 rule

This rule states that 80% of the effort goes into producing 20% of the results. This is true for most businesses, as 20% of the customers account for 80% of the sales. For example, in a pub, 20% of the customers, the regulars, will provide 80% of the sales. This is because costs are spread evenly across all customers, but a large percentage of time and resources is spent on the bottom 20% of customers. This is often used to justify additional staff and what is often needed is a system to reduce activity on the 20% of customers.

Break even

Many small businesses find it difficult to survive because too much start-up capital is used to buy fixed assets. Some equipment is essential in the beginning; others could be postponed. Some equipment can be hired or borrowed for a period, e.g., photocopiers, vehicles, etc. The higher the fixed costs, the longer it takes to reach break even. New businesses do not have time on their side; they need to break even quickly, otherwise they will run out of money. Break-even is important in preparing the business plan and in day-to-day decisions.

Fixed costs are those that stay the same irrespective of the number of units sold. Rent and business rates, for example, are constant and will be the same every month. Costs for resale, on the other hand, are dependent on the volume of goods or services sold. The former costs are fixed and the latter are called variable costs and, together, they make up the total costs. The higher the fixed costs, the longer it will take to reach break-even.

Harvesting strategy

When an entrepreneur aims to maximise profitability and cash flow in the short term, this can be described as a harvesting strategy. When a business is started, the main strategy is survival and then growth and, during the early

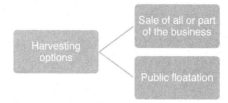

Figure 7.4 Harvesting options

stages, a harvesting strategy may not be considered. In a harvest strategy, the entrepreneur will reinvest as little as possible in order to maintain market share. Some entrepreneurs will harvest from their businesses not only to improve their own wealth, but also to give back to society.

In the short-term, a harvesting strategy can mean any form of extracting profits, including selling all or part of the business (Figure 7.4). For most entrepreneurs, it can take many years of hard work before they can consider a harvesting strategy. Many entrepreneurs get satisfaction from starting and running a business and may get less enjoyment once the business gets bigger. However, some entrepreneurs will have a harvesting strategy in mind when they start their business. Having a harvesting strategy from the beginning can provide motivation to build a good business, as the businesses that are designed to add value will develop new products and services and possibly be more innovative.

A stock market flotation involves selling a percentage of the business in the form of shares on the stock market. There are three stock markets in the UK. The main one is the London Stock Exchange, which is generally for large companies. The other two markets are aimed specifically at smaller companies – the Alternative Investment Market and PLUS. The Alternative Investment Market helps smaller and growing companies raise finance for expansion. AIM is part of the London Stock Exchange and is more flexible and has less regulation than the main market. Companies can move from AIM to the main market and vice versa.

Exit strategies

There are different types of entrepreneurial exit. Entrepreneurs running successful businesses may want to exit, possibly for personal reasons such as retirement, or low performing firms that have to be sold or liquidated in distress. If the business is making losses, then the entrepreneur may decide to sell or close the business. If a window of opportunity is missed to sell a

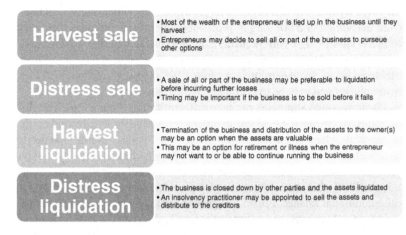

Figure 7.5 Sale and liquidation options

business, then disaster may strike. The 2008 credit crunch, for example, saw many businesses go into receivership or liquidation. Exit strategies can take many forms, as shown in Figure 7.5.

These strategies can often depend on factors such as the age of the entrepreneur. Older entrepreneurs are more likely to look for exit strategies when they are close to retirement, especially if there are no family members willing to take on running the business. Other factors, such as the level of education, may influence their decision, especially if there are other employment opportunities. If there are external investors, then it is less likely that the entrepreneur will liquidate the business.

Turnaround strategies

The failure rate for new ventures is relatively high, with around half going out of business within the first few years. The failure rate can be affected by both internal and external factors, including economic and political factors, although some of the reasons could be attributed to the entrepreneur's lack of financial and management skills. Poor financial management leading to cash-flow problems and failing to make sufficient sales can cause serious problems. Some businesses will recover and this section looks at recovery strategies.

The entrepreneur who has started the business may have a high degree of risk in that they have invested all their assets in the business. Undercapitalisation and over-reliance on short-term borrowing can increase the financial pressure. Failure, therefore, may have a catastrophic impact on them and they will try to avoid this if possible. However, this may also prevent them from delegating and bringing in professional managers, because they want to retain control. The entrepreneurs may also blame external organisations such as the banks for not providing additional funds when they are in trouble. In addition, some entrepreneurs may have an exaggerated view of their own abilities and may be over-reliant on their gut instinct.

The turnaround strategies can take different forms (Figure 7.6). The first option is to contract the business in order to reduce costs. The second option is survival, where the entrepreneur keeps the business going in order to turn the business around. The third is stability, which is a relatively passive approach in that the aim is to stay at the same level of operations and maintain the level of income. This may also give the entrepreneur more time to raise additional finance. Pursuing a growth strategy may appear to be counterintuitive. However, many entrepreneurs have traded out of a financial crisis by an expansion strategy. This option has the advantage of increasing sales and has the potential to improve profitability.

Running a business can be hard work and many entrepreneurs thrive on the challenge. If the business is successful, then the effort will be rewarded. However, in situations where the losses are accumulating and the debt is increasing, or when there are insufficient sales to make the business viable, the entrepreneur may consider other options. These can include taking a new job, retiring or closing the business down to focus on other, more profitable

Contraction	• Reduce the size of the business • Cut costs • Lay off staff
Survival	• Restore profitability • Improve cashflow • Improve competitiveness • Increase sales
Stability	• Passive approach • Aimed at staying the same • Maintain income
Growth	• Expansion • Increase sales • Improve profitability

Figure 7.6 Turnaround strategies

ventures. There are many examples of entrepreneurs, such as Tommy Hilfiger and Simon Cowell, who have attributed their success the second time around to the lessons learnt when they lost everything with their first business.

References

Bhide, A. (1992). Bootstrap finance: The art of start-ups. *Harvard Business Review*, *70*(6), 109–117.

Douglas, E. J. (2013). Reconstructing entrepreneurial intentions to identify predisposition for growth. *Journal of Business Venturing*, *28*(5), 633–651.

Lewis, V.L. and Churchill, N.C. (1983). 'The five stages of small business growth'. Harvard Business Reviw. *61*(3), 30–50.

Porter, M. E. (1980). *Competitive strategy: Techniques for analyzing industries and competitors*. New York. Free Press.

Stokes, D. (2000). Putting entrepreneurship into marketing: The process of entrepreneurial marketing. *Journal of Research into Marketing and Entrepreneurship*, *2*(1), 1–16.

Index

Note: Page numbers in *italics* indicate a figure and page numbers in **bold** indicate a table on the corresponding page.

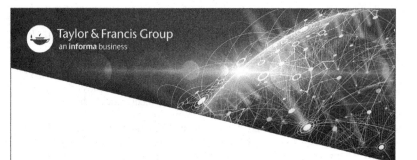

Taylor & Francis Group
an **informa** business

Taylor & Francis eBooks

www.taylorfrancis.com

A single destination for eBooks from Taylor & Francis
with increased functionality and an improved user
experience to meet the needs of our customers.

90,000+ eBooks of award-winning academic content in
Humanities, Social Science, Science, Technology, Engineering,
and Medical written by a global network of editors and authors.

TAYLOR & FRANCIS EBOOKS OFFERS:

A streamlined
experience for
our library
customers

A single point
of discovery
for all of our
eBook content

Improved
search and
discovery of
content at both
book and
chapter level

REQUEST A FREE TRIAL
support@taylorfrancis.com

 Routledge
Taylor & Francis Group

 CRC Press
Taylor & Francis Group